# 1001 Persian-English Proverbs

# One Thousand & One Persian-English Proverbs

*Learning Language and Culture
Through Commonly Used Sayings*

*Third Edition*

Compiled & Illustrated
by
Simin K. Habibian

IBEX PUBLISHERS
Bethesda, Maryland

One Thousand and One Persian-English Proverbs
collected and illustrated by Simin Habibian
Completely Revised Third Edition

هزار و یک مثل فارسی ــ انگلیسی

گردآوری و تصاویر از سیمین حبیبیان

Copyright © 1995, 1999, 2002 Simin Habibian

Cover illustration by Simin Habibian

Manufactured in the United States of America

The paper used in this book meets the minimum requirements of the American National Standard for Information Services—Permanence of Paper for Printed Library Materials, ANSI Z39.48-1984

IBEX Publishers, Inc.
Post Office Box 30087
Bethesda, Maryland 20824
telephone: 301-718-8188
facsimile: 301-907-8707
www.ibexpub.com

Library of Congress Cataloging in Publication Data

Hazar va yak masal-i Farsi-Ingilisi / girdavari va tasavir az Simin K. Habibiyan ; pishguftar az Manuchihr Aryanpur Kashani. -- Virast-i 3.

p. cm.

Cover title: 1001 masal-i Farsi-Ingilisi.

Added t.p. title: One thousand & one Persian-English proverbs.

Includes bibliographical reerences and index.

ISBN 1-58814-021-0 (alk. paper)

1. Proverbs, Persian. 2. Proverbs, Persian--Translations into English. 3. Proverbs, English. 4. Proverbs. English--Translations into Persian. I. Title: 1001 masal-i Farsi-Ingilisi. II. Title: One thousand & one Persian-English proverbs. III. Title: One thousand and one Persian-English proverbs.

PN6519.P5 H39 2002
398.9'9155--dc21                                        2002022207

*For Taghi*

# TABLE OF CONTENTS

*On Persian side of book*

# FOREWORD BY SHUSHA GUPPY

Simin Habibian's wonderful compilation of Persian proverbs and their English counterparts is a treasure trove of timeless wit, wisdom and poetry. Proverbs are the expression of a people's journey through innocence to experience, and they provide an insight into its collective soul. Persian and English belong to the same family of languages, and by bringing together Persian proverbs and their English twins Simin Habibian demonstrates the similarities between two ancient communities at the deepest level, beyond geographical and historical divides. They belie Rudyard Kipling's pessimistic view that "East is East and West Is West and never the twain shall meet" — they meet in the pages of this charming, humorous book, and have a good deal of fun together and with us.

At a time when so much nonsense is written about the "clash of civilisations", and the differences between various cultures and traditions are emphasised, it is salutary to point out what connects us in our common humanity, to dissipate mistrust and generate affection. Ms. Habibian does this with remarkable lightness of touch. Her own tongue-in-cheek illustrations enhance the humour of the maxims and adages. All this makes her collection a delicious treat for both Persian and English-speaking readers.

— Shusha Guppy, London.

# INTRODUCTION

A cultural gap is growing between the adults and children of Iranian families residing outside of Iran. Young Iranians are strongly influenced by Western culture, while the adults struggle with Western culture and try to maintain their homeland's traditions. A bridge is needed to overcome this gap. The first edition of *One Thousand and One Persian-English Proverbs* was written with this goal in mind and was published in August 1996. The book focused on the similarities, rather than the differences, that exist between commonly used English and Persian proverbs. Its message was that both cultures have thousands of years of similar experiences and share in the wisdom collected over this time.

IBEX Publisher now publishes this third edition of the book with several improvements over its previous editions. Since English is the first language of the majority of the readers of this book, changes have been made to better accommodate them. However, the intention of this book still remains the closing the cultural gap within the Iranian-American family and between the Iranian and American communities. This obviously is a difficult task; but "a journey of a thousand miles begins with the first step."

My journey in the universe of proverbs started the same way. After leaving Iran in 1981, our family settled in Silver Spring, Maryland. Soon after that I volunteered to teach Persian to young English speaking Iranians at the first Persian community school in the area. In conversing with my students as well as my own children, I discovered that reciting Persian proverbs was a very effective teaching method. To make sure that they understood the meaning of a Persian proverb, I immediately followed it by a similar English one. I also found that using a pictorial proverb quiz like the ones I have in the book helped the student to learn and understand the language faster, while also having fun.

Over the years I noted with amazement much similarities between the proverbs of the two countries. Sometimes the similarities of the proverbs were so close that one could easily be mistaken as the translation of the other. For example, in Persian it is said: "If God closes a door, he opens another." The English equivalent of this proverb is: "If God closes a door, he opens a window." A Persian proverb states: "It is not by saying halva, halva, that sweetness will come to mouth." Its English equivalent is: "It is not by saying honey, honey that sweetness will come into mouth".

The significant similarities between many of the Persian and English proverbs was exciting and led me to believe that proverbs can also be used to reduce the generational gap between Iranian adults and the newer generation living outside Iran. Proverbs can minimize the language and cultural barrier between parents and children and provide them with a useful communication tool. The similarities also led me to think about the origin of the proverb in a historical perspective.

Webster defines a proverb as: "A short, traditional saying that expresses some obvious truth or similar experiences." Proverbs are rich in meaning and communicate much with few words. Despite this, proverbs did not seem to me only as short, interesting phrases used to ornament conversation. They are also symbolic of the history and culture of a people, representing the expressions of centuries of experiences of our ancestors and revealing much about their world view.

With such excitement, the idea of compiling a book on proverbs came to me. I started to write down the similar Persian-English proverbs I knew and started searching for others. This took me several years. It was such an interesting and addicting experience. I carried the proverbs with me everywhere; I worked with them; drove with them, slept with them, and talked and dreamt about them. I also lost quite a few pounds because of them! I am proud of my effort and very pleased with the outcome. I have been able to publicize one aspect of Iranian and American culture in an understandable format for the general reader.

Similar Persian and English proverbs are not limited to the ones I have included in this book. The more I looked for English equivalents of Persian proverbs, the more I found. But I had to stop somewhere. Recalling the lovely stories of Princess Scheherazade in the "1001 Nights," well known to both Iranians and Americans, I stopped at a thousand and added one of my own: "May 1001 proverbs bring you delight, more than the stories of the 1001 nights."

Obviously similarities between proverbs are not universal and without exception. Some of the experiences are common to many cultures and some are not, and so go the proverbs. A comparative study of Chinese and American proverbs at Ohio State University concluded that Americans take more risks in social situations than do the Chinese. This matches well with individualistic attitude prevailing among Americans. Despite such differences, similarities of proverbs are abundant. Noting the many similarities that exist between Persian and Western proverbs, and thus culture, brings us to an understanding that regardless of the nation we live in, we are all human and share similar experiences in our lives. This understanding hopefully can narrow the gap between us. The conflict between civilizations can, hopefully, be transformed to peace.

We, Iranian-Americans, are trying to preserve and respect our native culture and traditions, and transfer them to the next generation. Sometimes this is done by criticizing and emphasizing the shortcomings of the West. This drives the young away from us. In studying proverbs I have noted and emphasized the similarities. I hope that this commonality would help us to appreciate better and feel more attached to our new home. I also hope that our fellow Americans can see us, the Iranian-American, in a new light and as part of their community.

The proverbs have been arranged alphabetically in Persian. The first line is the Persian proverb; the nearest English equivalent of each proverb follows immediately. Below that, in italics, is the literal translation of the Persian proverb. When the English and Persian are similar, no literal translation has been provided. The literal translations show the cultural setting of Persian proverbs and will help those with limited or no familiarity with Persian language or culture.

Seventy-one new pictorial quiz proverbs have been added to this third edition. The quiz illustrations are numbered and the equivalents or corresponding proverbs, which are literal translations of the Persian version of each proverb, are listed in the answer section. Most of the illustrations depict those proverbs that are near equivalents in English and Persian; the rest are based on Persian proverbs.

I would like to thank all my friends who have helped me with the first and second editions including, Manouchehr Aryanpour Kashani; M. Ali Aboughaddareh, Hadi Bahar, Farhad Falaki, Hasan Javadi, Jodye L. Russell, Esfandiar Sepehri; and my publisher, Farhad Shirzad. I am much indebted to all the readers whose support has encouraged me to continue in my cultural work. I am also grateful to the Persian language and American media for their help in promoting this book.

I wish to appreciate the help of Shusha Guppy, singer, and author of *The Blindfold Horse*; Salar Abdoh, author of *The Poet Game*; Hadi Khorsandi, the great satirist; Barbara Slavin, of *USA Today* and Ellen Sciolino of *The New York Times* who read and commented on this book.

Finally, I wish to thank my husband Taghi, for his support and patience; my son Pouya; and my daughter Mahtab, who have been my greatest inspiration in compiling this book.

— Simin Habibian, Silver Spring.
March, 2002

# The
# Proverbs

آب از سرچشمه گل آلود است.

An ill beginning, an ill ending.
*The water is turbid from it's source.*

آب از سرش گذشته.

The water has risen over his head.

آب در کوزه و ما تشنه لبان می گردیم.

We seek water in the sea.
*While there is water in the pitcher, we wander thirsty.*

آب در گوش ریختن.

To throw dust in someone's eyes.
*To put water in someone's ear.*

آب در هاون کوبیدن.

To carry water in a sieve.
*To pound water in a mortar.*

آب ریخته جمع شدنی نیست.

Don't cry over spilled milk.
*Spilled water cannot be gathered again.*

آب رفته به جوی باز نمی گردد.

What is done cannot be undone.
*The water that has run down the stream will not return.*

آبشان به یک جوی نمی رود.

Oil and water don't mix.
*Their water does not flow in one stream.*

آب که از سر گذشت چه یک نی چه صد نی.

As well be hanged for a sheep as for a lamb.
*When water rises above one's head, it doesn't matter whether one foot or a hundred.*

آب که یکجا بماند می گندد.

Standing pools gather filth.
*Still water spoils.*

1

آدم به امید زنده است.

Hope keeps man alive.

آدم تا کوچکی نکند به بزرگی نمی رسد.

To learn to command one must learn to obey.
*Until a man has not humbled himself, he cannot reach greatness.*

2

آدم تا مریض نشود قدر سلامتی را نمی داند.

Health is not valued until sickness comes.
*One does not know the value of health until one is sick.*

آدم ترسو همیشه جان سالم بدر می برد.

Better a coward for a minute than dead for the rest of your life.
*The coward always survives.*

آدم ترسو روزی هزار بار می میرد.

Cowards die many times before their death.
*Cowards die a thousand times.*

آدم تنبل بهانه گیر هم می شود.

Idle folks lack no excuses.
*Lazy folks lack no excuses.*

آدم دانا به نیشتر نزند مشت.

A wise man avoids edged tools.

آدم دروغگو کم حافظه است.

A liar should have a good memory.
*A liar has a short memory.*

آدم زرنگ پایش روی پوست خربزه بند است.

Good swimmers are oftenest drowned.
*A man who is too clever has his foot on a melon skin.*

آدم عاقل دوبار گول نمی خورد.

Fool me once shame on you, fool me twice, shame on me.
*A wise man will not be deceived twice.*

آدم عجول کار را دوبار می کند.

Hasty work, double work.

آدم که قحط نیست.

There are plenty of fish in the sea.
*There is no scarcity of people.*

آدم گرسنه دین و ایمان ندارد.

A hungry man, an angry man.
*A hungry belly has no faith.*

4

آدمی را عقل می باید نه زور.

Wisdom is better than strength.
*One needs wisdom not strength.*

آدم گرسنه سنگ را هم می خورد.

Hunger makes hard beans sweet.
*A hungry man would even eat stone.*

آدم گدا اینهمه ادا؟

Beggars can't be choosers.
*A beggar cannot be fussy.*

آدم لخت خواب کرباس دولا پهنا می بیند.

The cat dreams of mice.
*A naked man dreams of a double-width cloth.*

آدم یکدفعه به دنیا می آید، یکدفعه هم از دنیا می رود.

He that is once born, once must die.
*Man is born once and will die once.*

آرامش قبل از طوفان.

It is always calm before the storm.
*The calm before the storm.*

آرد خود را بیختیم و غربال خود را آویختیم.

Hang up one's sword.
*I have sifted my flour and hung up the sieve.*

آرزو سرمایۀ مفلس است.

Hope is the poor man's bread.
*The wish is the poor man's wealth.*

آری به اتفاق جهان می توان گرفت.

In union there is strength.
*United, we seize the world.*

6

آزمند همیشه نیازمند است.

The miser is always in want.
*A greedy person is always in need.*

آسمان بزمین نمیاد.

It will not make the sky fall.
*The sky will not fall.*

آسوده کسی که خر ندارد

از کاه و جواش خبر ندارد

Little wealth, little care.
*Lucky is he who has no mule,*
*who does not have to worry about it's hay and barley.*

آسه برو، آسه بیا که گربه شاخت نزنه.

He that goes softly, goes safely.
*Go softly, come softly, so that the cat does not gore you.*

آسیا به نوبت.

First come, first served.
*One must take his turn in the mill.*

7

آش خودت را هم بزن.

Inquire not what boils in another's pot.
*Stir your own soup.*

آش دهن سوزی نیست.

It is nothing to write home about.
*It is not a soup to burn the mouth.*

آشپز که دو تا شد آش یا شور می شود یا بی نمک.

Too many cooks spoil the broth.
*When the cooks are two, the soup will be too salty or saltless.*

آشی برات بپزم که روش یک وجب روغن بایسته.

I will blow you sky high.
*I'll cook you a soup with lots of oil on top of it.*

آفتاب لب بام است.

He has one foot in the grave.
*He is the sunshine at the edge of the roof.*

آفتابه خرج لحیم.

The game is not worth the candle.
*The pitcher has to be sold to pay for its soldering.*

آفتاب از کدام طرف در آمده؟

Once in a blue moon.
*From which side did the sun rise?*

آمد به سرم از آنچه می ترسیدم.

That which one most anticipates, soonest comes to pass.
*The very thing I feared befell me.*

8

9

آمد زیر ابروش را برداره، چشمش را هم کور کرد.

Striving to better, often we mar what is well.
*Trying to pluck her eyebrows, she blinded herself.*

آمدی جانم به قربانت ولی حالا چرا؟

While the grass grows, the horse starves.
*Oh dear, you arrived, but why so late?*

آنان که غنی ترند محتاج ترند.

The more you get the more you want.
*They who have more, need more.*

آنچه در دل است به زبان می آید.

What the heart thinks the tongue speaks.
*What is in the heart, comes to the tongue.*

آنچه دلم خواست نه آن می شود، آنچه خدا خواست همان می شود.

All must be as God wills.
*What I wanted did not happen, what God willed happened.*

آنچه شیـــــران را کند روبه مزاج

احتیاج است احتیاج است، احتیاج

Hunger will tame a lion.
*What gives the lion the nature of a fox is necessity, necessity,*
*and necessity.*

آن درسی را که تو خوندی ما از بریم.

You need not teach fish to swim.
*The lesson you just read, we knew by heart.*

10

آن دو شاخ گاو اگـر خر داشتی

یک شـــکم در آدمی نگذاشتی

Fools should not have a chopping stick.
*If the ass had two horns of the ox, there would not be any guts*
*(life) in anyone.*

آن سبو بشکست و آن پیمانه ریخت.

The mill cannot grind with water that is past.
*That jar broke and the wine spilled.*

آنرا که حساب پاک است از محاسبه چه باک است.

A clear conscience fears not false accusation.

آنقدر بار کن که بکِشَد، نه آنقدر که بکُشَد.

The straw that broke the camel's back.
*Load as much as can be carried, not as much that can kill.*

آنکس که به عیب خلق پرداخته اسـت

ز آنست که عیب خویش نشناخته است

The eye that sees all things, sees not itself.
*He who speaks of other's faults does not know his own faults.*

آنکـس که نداند و بداند که نـــداند

لنگان خرک خویش به منزل برساند

To be conscious that you're ignorant is a great step to knowledge.
*He who knows he does not know will eventually bring his
limping donkey home.*

آنکه باد بکارد، طوفان درو می کند.

He who sow the wind shall reap the whirlwind.

آن ممه را لولو برد.

That is all past and done.
*The bogeyman has carried off that breast.*

آنور سکه را هم باید دید.

Every medal has a reverse.
*The other side of the coin has to be seen.*

آن نوش به این نیش نمی ارزد.

Honey is sweet, but the bee stings.
*That sweetness is not worth this sting.*

آنها دو نفر بودند همراه، ما صد نفر بودیم تنها.

United we stand, divided we fall.
*They were two, but united; we were a hundred but divided.*

12

آواز دهل شنیدن از دور خوش است.

Far fowls have fair feather.
*The sound of the drum is pleasant at a distance.*

آواز سگان کم نکند رزق گدا را.

Sticks and stones may break my bones, but words will never hurt me.
*The barking of dogs does not reduce the beggar's daily allotment.*

13

آه ندارد که با ناله سودا کند.

He is as poor as a church mouse.
*He has not even a sigh to exchange for groan.*

آینه داری در مجلس کوران.

Blind man will not thank you for a looking glass.
*To hold up a mirror in the assembly of the blind.*

**ابرو گشاده باش چو دستت گشاده نیست.**

He that has not silver in his purse should have silk in his tongue.
*If you cannot be open handed, be open browed.*

**ابلهی گفت و احمقی باور کرد.**

A fool believes everything.
*A stupid person says one thing and another believes.*

**اتاقی که آفتاب در آن وارد نشود، دکتر وارد می شود.**

Where the sun enters, the doctor does not.
*The room where the sun does not enter, the doctor will.*

**احتیاج مادر اختراع است.**

Necessity is the mother of invention.

**احمدک نه دردی داشت نه بیماری، سوزنی به خود می زد و می نالید.**

He that has no ill fortune, is troubled with good.
*Little Ahmad had no pain or disease, he poked himself with a needle and whimpered!*

**ادب از که آموختی، از بی ادبان.**

A fool may give a wise man counsel.
*Where did you learn manners? From the ill mannered.*

ارزان خری، انبان خری.

Don't buy everything that is cheap.
*Buying cheap is buying rubbish.*

از آب کره گرفتن.

To skin a flint.
*To get butter from water.*

از آب گل آلود باید ماهی گرفت.

It is good fishing in troubled water.
*In muddy waters one must catch fish.*

14

از آن بیدها نیست که با این بادها بلرزد.

He has lived too near a wood to be frightened by owls.
*He is not one of those willows that tremble at these winds.*

از آن نترس که های و هو دارد

از آن بترس که سر به تــو دارد

Great barkers are no biters.
*Do not fear him who makes an outcry, but fear him who keeps his head down.*

15

از او آبی گرم نمی شود.

Don't count on him.
*He won't heat any water.*

از این گوش می شنود و از آن گوش در می کند.

Go in one ear and out the other.

از بزرگان عفو باشد از فرودستان گناه.

The noblest vengeance is to forgive.
*Inferiors sin, superiors forgive.*

از برهنه پوستین چون برکنی.

It is hard to shave an egg.
*Taking a coat off a naked man.*

از بیکاری مگس می پراند.

The dog that is idle barks at his fleas.
*He swats flies from idleness.*

16

از چاله در آمدن و به چاه افتادن.

Out of the frying pan and into the fire.
*To come out of the ditch and to fall into the well.*

از خرس یک مو هم غنیمت است.

Take rough oats of a bad debtor.
*A hair from a bear is worth a treasure.*

از خوشی در پوست خود نمی گنجد.

He is happy as a clam.
*He is bursting out of his skin from joy.*

از درد لاعلاجی به گربه میگه خانباجی.

Call the bear "uncle" until you're safe across the bridge.
*Out of desperation he calls the cat "Madam!"*

از دل برود هر آنکه از دیده برفت.

Far from eye, far from heart.

از دور دل میبرد و از نزدیک زهره را.

Distance lends enchantment to the view.
*Afar, it enraptures the heart, when near, it rends the gallbladder.*

از دوست یک اشارت، از من به سر دویدن.

Your wish is my command.
*A single gesture from you and I'll be running to you.*

از سه چیزباید ترسید دیوار شکسته، سگ درنده و زن سلیطه.

Three things cost dear: the caresses of a dog, the love of a whore, and the invitation of a host.
*Three things to fear: a crumbling wall, an angry dog, and a shrew.*

از شما عباسی، از ما رقاصی.

You buy, I fly.
*From you the money (Abbasi), from me the dance.*

از شوره زمین سمن نروید.

Of a thorn springs not a fig.
*A jasmine flower will not grow in salty ground.*

18

از قسمت نمیشود فرار کرد.

Flee never so fast you cannot flee your fortune.
*You cannot flee fortune.*

از کاه کوهی ساختن.

Making a mountain out of a molehill.
*Making a mountain out of hay.*

از کوزه همان برون تراود که در اوست.

There comes not out of the sack but what was there.
*What comes out of a jug is what's in it.*

**از کیسهٔ خلیفه می بخشد.**

He is free of fruit that wants an orchard.
*He gives away from the caliph's purse.*

**از گرگ شبانی نیاید.**

It is an ill sign to see a fox become a shepherd.
*It does not become the wolf to be a shepherd.*

**از گیر دزد درآمدن و گیر رمال افتادن.**

Out of the frying pan and into the fire.
*To escape the thief and fall into the hands of the soothsayer.*

**از مخ معاف است.**

He is off his rocker.
*He is free of brain.*

19

**از مکافات عمل غافل مشو.**

Chickens come home to roost.
*Don't neglect the consequence of your act.*

از من گفتن و از تو نشنیدن.

In vain he craves advice that he will not follow.
*My saying and your not listening.*

ازین ستون به آن ستون فرج است.

He that has time has life.
*From one pillar to the other, there is relief.*

اسب نجیب را یک تازیانه بس است.

A running horse needs no spur.
*A submitting horse needs only one whip.*

20

اسب و خر را که یکجا ببندند، اگر هم بو نشوند، هم خو خواهند شد.

If you lie down with dogs, you will get up with fleas.
*A horse and an ass tied side by side become of the same temperament, though not of the same odor.*

اسب و استر به هم لگد نزنند.

There is honor among thieves.
*Horse and mule do not kick each other.*

21

اسبی را که در چهل سالگی سوغان گیرند میدان قیامت را شاید.

You can't teach an old dog new tricks.
*A horse which is tamed at forty is only good for resurrection day.*

اشکش تو مشکش است.

To weep crocodile tears.
*His tears are in his sleeves.*

اصل بد نیکو نگردد آنکه بنیادش بد است.

The leopard cannot change his spot.
*One of bad origin will not become good.*

افاده ها طبق طبق، سگها به دورش وّق و وّق.

A proud mind and a beggar's purse agree not together.

اگر به هر سر مویت دو صد هنر باشد

هنر به کــار نیاید چـو بخت بـد باشد

It is better to be lucky than wise.
*Should you have two hundred talents hung from your hair they are useless if the fortune is adverse.*

اگر بیل زنی باغچه خودت را بیل بزن.

Physician, heal thyself.
*If you are a digger, dig your own garden.*

22

اگر پیش همه روسیاهم، پیش دزد روسفیدم.

A clear conscience fears not false accusation.
*If everybody accuses me of stealing, At least the one who stole knows that he did it.*

اگر تنگدستی مرو پیش یار

وگر سیم داری بیا و بیـــــار

Money makes marriage.
*If you are poor don't go to your sweetheart, if you have money go to her and take the money with you.*

اگر تو را زر باشد عالمیت برادر باشد.

Wealth makes many friends.
*If you have got money the world is your brother.*

23

اگر خواهی شوی خوشنویس، بنویس، بنویس، بنویس.

Practice makes perfect.
*If you want to be a good writer, write, write and write.*

اگر دیده نبیند دل نخواهد.

What the eye does not see the heart does not grieve over.
*If the eye does not see, the heart does not desire.*

اگر را با مگر تزویج کردند از آنان بچه ای شدکاشکی نام.

If wishes were horses, then beggars would ride.
*When "If" and "perhaps" get married the offspring is just a wish.*

اگر رویه بدی آسترش را هم میخاد.

Give him an inch and he'll take a yard.
*If you give him a coat, he would ask for the lining.*

اگر زری بپوشی، اگر اطلس بپوشی، همان کنگر فروشی!

Clothes don't make the man.
*If you dress in gold or silk, you are still the same green grocer.*

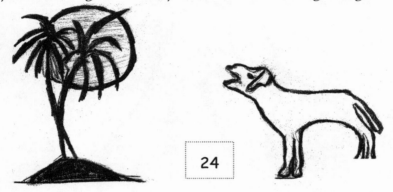

24

اگر علی ساربونه، میدونه شترشو کجا بخوابونه.

Every man knows his own business best.
*If Ali is the camel driver, he knows where to make his camel kneel.*

اگر لرُ به بازار نره بازار می گنده.

If fools went not to market, bad wares wouldn't be sold.
*If a Luri* does not go to market, all the goods would spoil.*

---

*A man from Lurestan.

اگر سر آزار داری بهانه بسیار داری.

Give a dog an ill name and hang him.
*If you want to abuse, you have plenty of excuse.*

اگر نخوری همیشه داری.

He that saves his dinner will have the more for his supper.
*If you don't eat it, you will always have it.*

الهی مرا آن دِه که مرا بِه.

If God does not give us what we want, he gives us what we need.
*Oh, God, give me what is good for me.*

25

امروز و فردا کردن.

One of these days is none of these days.
*Putting off things from today to tomorrow.*

امیدوار بود آدمی به خیر کســـــان

مرا به خیر تو امید نیست شرّ مرسان

If you can't say something nice, don't say anything.
*Man hopes for good from others; I hope for no good from you;*
*do me no harm.*

26

اندازه نگهدار که اندازه نکوست.

True happiness springs from moderation.
*Be moderate, for moderation is good*

اندر این خاکدان فرسوده

هیچکس را نبینی آسوده

No day passes without some grief.
*No one is without grief.*

اندک اندک بهم شود بسیار

دانه دانه است غله در انبـــار

Many a little makes a mickle.[*]
*Little will make much, as the granary is made of single grains.*

اندک دان بسیار گوست.

Foolish tongues talks by the dozen.
*He who knows little, talks much.*

اندکی جمال به از بسیاری مال.

Beauty opens locked doors.
*A little beauty is better than much property.*

27

اندیشه کردن که چه گویم به از پشیمانی خوردن که چرا گفتم.

He thinks not well that thinks not again.
*Better to think about what to say than to regret saying it.*

---

[*] Much.

**انگار از دماغ فیل افتاده.**

He is as proud as a peacock.
*It's as if she's fallen off an elephant's trunk.*

**انگور خوب نصیب شغال می شود.**

Into the mouth of a bad dog, often falls a good bone.
*Fine grapes fall to the lot of the jackal.*

**اوزوم\* و انگور.**

Six of one, a half a dozen of the other.
*Grapes and grapes!*

**اول اندیشه وانگهی گفتار.**

Think before you speak.
*First think, then speak.*

28

**اول چاه را بکن، بعد منار را بدزد.**

You're a fool to steal, if you can't conceal.
*Do not steal the minaret before you have dug a pit to hide it in.*

---

\*لغت ترکی انگور است.

اول خویش، بعد درویش.

A man should keep from the blind and give to his kin.
*First your own, then the poor.*

29

اول همسایه را بپرس بعد خانه را بخر.

First, ask about your neighbor, then buy the house.

احمق آن است که بـــــالاتر نشست

استخوانش سخت تر خواهد شکست

Climb not too high lest the fall be greater.
*The higher the fool sits, the greater the fall will be.*

ای آقای کمر باریک کوچه روشن کن و خانه تاریک.

He hangs his fiddle when he comes home.
*Don't keep the alley light and your own house dark!*

ای بسا اسب تیـزرو که بمرد

خرک لنگ جان به منزل برد

Fair and softly goes far.
*Many a swift horse died, but the lame ass arrived safely home.*

**ای من فدای آنکه دلش با زبان یکی است.**

It is a good tongue that says no ill, and a better heart that thinks none.

*I die for whom his heart and tongue speak the same.*

**این به آن در.**

Tit for tat.

30

**این حرفها برای فاطی تنبون نمیشه.**

Fair words fill not the belly.

*All this talk will not make pants for Fati.\**

**این دم شیر است به بازی مگیر.**

Don't play with fire.

*That is the lion's tail, do not play with it.*

**این دیگ را این چغندر سزاست.**

As the bird is, such is the nest.

*Such a beet for such a pot.*

---

\* A girl's name.

این دغل دوستان که می بینی

مگسانند گرد شیرینـــــــی

Dogs wag their tails not so much in love to you as to your bread.
*All these fake friends that you see are like flies around sweets.*

این رشته سر دراز دارد.

It is a long story.
*This string has no end.*

31

این ره که تو میروی به ترکستان است.

What is the use of running when you're on the wrong road.
*This road you are on goes to Turkestan.*

این کار دل است نه خشت و گل.

Love is not found in the market.
*This is a work of the heart, not of mud and mortar.*

32

ای گرفتارو پای بــند عیال

دگر آسودگـی مبند خیال

Needles and pins, needles and pins; when a man marries his trouble begins.
*Oh you who have sought a wife, forget about peace of mind.*

این نیز بگذرد.

Time is a great healer.
*This too will pass.*

با آنکه خصومت نتوان کرد بساز.

If you can't beat them, join them.
*If you can't be an enemy, get along.*

با پنبه سر می برد.

To kill a man with a cushion.
*He cuts one's head with cotton.*

با «حلوا حلوا» گفتن دهن شیرین نمیشه.

It is not by saying honey, honey, that sweetness will come into mouth.
*The mouth does not become sweet by saying, "halvah, halvah."**

با خود لجبازی کردن.

To cut off your nose to spite your face.
*To be obstinate to oneself.*

با خودی معامله خطاست.

Do no business with kinsman.
*It is a mistake to do business with kin.*

---

* A sweet.

باد آورده را باد می برد.

Easy come easy go.
*What the wind brings, the wind takes.*

33

با دست پس می زند با پا پیش می کشد.

He refuses with the right hand and takes with the left.
*He refuses with his hand, but pulls it with his foot.*

بادنجان بد آفت ندارد.

A bad vessel is seldom broken.
*No plague will come to a bad eggplant.*

با دوستان دوست ترا دوستی نکوست.

Friends of my friends are also friends.

با دوستان مروت با دشمنان مدارا.

Have patience with a friend rather than lose him forever.
*Tolerance for friends, mercy for enemies.*

بار کج به منزل نمی رسد.

Honesty is the best policy.
*Slanting baggage never reaches home.*

بارک الله قبای کسی را رنگین نکند.

Praise without profit puts little in the pot.
*"Praise" will not make a man's cloak colorful.*

با زبون خوش می شود مار را از سوراخ بیرون کشید.

A single kind word keeps one warm for three months.
*A kind word can bring out a snake out of a hole.*

بازگردد به اصل خود هر چیز.

Blood will tell.
*Everything goes back to its origin.*

34

باز ناید تیر هرگز کز کمان بیرون شود.

What's done cannot be undone.
*An arrow once shot will never return to the bow.*

بازوی بخت به که بازوی سخت.

Good luck reaches further than long arms.
*Good luck is better than a strong arm.*

بازی اشکنک داره، سر شکستنک داره.

If you play with fire, you will get burnt.
*When you play, you may break your head.*

35

با سرنوشت نمیشود بازی کرد.

No flying from fate.
*No playing with fate.*

باغبان را وقت میوه گوشها کر شود.

Harvest ears, thick of hearing.
*The gardener's ears become deaf at harvest.*

با گرگ دنبه می خورد، با چوپان گریه میکند.

No man can serve two masters.
*He eats sheep's fat with the wolf and weeps with the shepherd.*

با یک تیر دو نشان زدن.

Killing two birds with one stone.
*Hitting two targets with one stone.*

با یک دست دو هندوانه نمی شود برداشت.

If you run after two hares, you will catch neither.
*Two watermelons cannot be carried in one hand.*

با یک پرستو تابستان نمی آید.

One swallow does not a summer make.

36

با یک گل بهار نمی شود.

One flower makes no garden.
*One flower does not make spring.*

بپوش و بپاش و بنوش و بخور
ترا بهره اینست از این رهگذر

Eat, drink and be merry, for tomorrow we may die.

بجز کشتهٔ خویشتن ندروی.

As you sow, you shall mow.
*You can't reap, but what you sow.*

بچهٔ سر پیری زنگولهٔ پای تابوت است.

Late children, early orphans.
*Children at an old age is like a bell hung from the coffin.*

بخت که برگردد عروس در حجله نر گردد.

If anything can go wrong, it will.
*In bad fortune, the bride will turn male in her bridal chamber.*

37

بخت می‌آید ولی آدمی در خانه نیست.

Opportunity knocks but once.
*Good luck knocks, but no one is at home.*

بخشش از بزرگتر است و گناه از کوچکتر.

The noblest vengeance is to forgive.
*Inferiors sin, and superiors forgive.*

بخند، تا دنیا با تو بخندد.

Laugh and the world laughs with you.

38

بخیه به آبدوغ زدن.

To kick the wind.
*Stitching yogurt.*

بد نکن که بد بینی.

You reap what you sow.
*Don't do bad or it will befall you.*

بده و بستان.

Give and take is a fair play.
*Give and take.*

بر احـــوال آنکس بباید گریـــست
که دخلش بود نوزده، خرج بیست

One is never rich until he commences to keep ahead of his expenses.
*We must weep for he who makes nineteen and spends twenty.*

برای آدم بدبخت از در ودیوار می بارد.

When it rains it pours.
*For the unlucky, bad fortune pours from the doors and walls.*

39

برای لای جرز دیوارخوبه.

He is good for nothing.
*He is good for building material.*

برای پشیمانی هیچوقت دیر نیست.

It is never too late to repent.

برادری بجای خود بزغاله یکی هفت صنار.

Business is business.
*Forget brotherhood, each goat will cost you seven Dinars.*

برای کور تاریک و روشن یکسان است.

A pebble and a diamond are all alike to a blind man.
*To the blind, dark and light are the same.*

برای یادگرفتن هیچوقت دیر نیست.

Never too old to learn.

برای دگر روز چیزی بنه.

Keep something for a rainy day.

برای یک بی نماز در مسجد را نمی بندند.

For one that is missing, there is no spoiling a wedding.
*The mosque's door is not shut to he who does not pray.*

برای یک دستمال قیصریه را آتش نمی زنند.

Burn not your house to frighten the mouse away.
*You don't burn down the marketplace for the sake of a handkerchief.*

بر زبان بود مرا آنچه تو را در دل بود.

Take the words out of someone's mouth.
*What is in your heart is on my tongue.*

40

بر زخم کسی نمک پاشیدن.

To put one's finger in another's sore.
*To sprinkle salt on someone's wound.*

بر سنگ گردان نروید نبات.

A rolling stone gathers no moss.

41

بر گذشته حسرت خوردن خطاست.

Don't cry over spilled milk.
*It is a mistake to regret the past.*

بر گذشته ها صلوات.

Let bygones be bygones.

بر مال و جمال خویش مغرور مشو
کانرا به شـــبی و این را به تبـــــی

Beauty is skin deep.
*Don't pride over your wealth or beauty,*
*one will be gone in a night and the other with a fever.*

برو کار میکن مگوچیست کار

که سرمایهٔ جاودانی است کار

Diligence is the mother of good fortune.
*Work and don't complain, for work is the capital of immortality.*

برو کشکت را بساب.

Mind your own business.
*Go rub your own whey!*

برهنه باک ندارد ز راهزن.

A beggar can never be bankrupt.
*A poor man is not afraid of the thief.*

بزرگ آنکه او را بسی دشمن است.

If you have no enemies, it's a sign that fortune has forgotten you.
*A great man has many enemies.*

42

بزرگی به عقل است نه به سال.

Wisdom goes not always by years.
*Greatness goes by wisdom, not by years.*

بزک نمیر بهار میاد، کُمبزه با خیار میاد!

If the sky falls, we shall catch larks.
*Little goat, don't die. Spring is coming with melons and cucumbers.*

بسیار سفر باید تا پخته شود خامی.

Travel broadens the mind.
*One must travel to become experienced.*

بشر جایزالخطاست.

To err is human.
*Man is fallible.*

بشنو و باور مکن.

Believe not all you hear.
*Hear it, but don't believe it.*

43

بنی آدم اعضای یـکدیگــرند
که در آفرینش زیک گوهرند

Human blood is all of a color.
*Human beings are part of each other,*
*they are created from the same clay.*

بوی حلواش میاد.

He has one foot in the grave.
*You can smell his halvah.**

به بهانه بچه ننه میخوره قند و کلوچه.

Nurses put one bit in the child's mouth and two in their own.
*The child is an excuse for the mother to eat candies and*
*cookies.*

44

به حُسنت نناز که به یک تب بند است.

Beauty fades like a flower.
*Do not boast of your beauty, it will be marred by a single fever.*

---

* In Iran halvah is often served when someone dies.

به حرف گربه سیاه بارون نمیاد.

The prayers of the wicked won't prevail.
*The prayers of the black cat will not bring rain.*

به دشت آهوی ناگرفته مبخش.

It is ill fishing before the net.
*Don't give away the deer you have not caught.*

45

به راحتی نرسید آنکه زحمتی نکشید.

No pain, no gain.
*He who does not toil, attains not comfort.*

به زیاد بگیر تا به کم راضی بشی.

Ask much to have little.

بهشت زیر پای مادران است.

God could not be everywhere and, therefore, he made mothers.
*Heaven is under the feet of mothers.*

به شیرین زبانی و لطف و خوشی

توانی که فیلی به مویی کشــــی

Honey catches more flies than vinegar.
*With gentle words, kindness and joy, you can pull an elephant
by the hair.*

به صبر از غوره حلوا می توان ساخت.

Time and straw make meddlers ripe.
*With patience one can make halvah with sour grape.*

به عمل کار برآید به سخندانی نیست.

Action speaks louder than words.

46

به کچل گفتند چرا مو نمی گذاری گفت: ازین قرتی بازی ها خوشم نمیاد.

Foxes, when they cannot reach the grapes, say they are not
ripe.
*On being asked, "why don't you grow hair?" the bald man said,
"I don't like vain play."*

به هر کجا که روی آسمان همین رنگ است.

Nothing is new under the sun.
*Wherever you go, the sky is the same color.*

47

به گدا چه یک نان بدی چه بگیری.

He that has nothing needs fear to lose nothing.
*Taking or giving bread to a beggar.*

به گنجشکه گفتند منار به فلانت، گفت: یه چیزی بگو که بگنجه.

You can't get a quart into a pint.

به لقمان حکمت آموزی خطاست.

You need not teach fish to swim.
*It is a mistake to teach wisdom to Aesop.*

به همدیگر نان قرض می دهند.

Scratch my back and I'll scratch yours.
*They lend bread to each other.*

به یک جو نمی ارزد.

It is not worth a penny.
*It is not worth a grain of barley.*

به یک کرشمه دو کار کردن.

To kill two birds with one stone.
*Doing two things with one gesture.*

به یک دست نتوان گرفتن دو به.

No man can do two things at once.
*You can't hold two quinces in one hand.*

بی خبری، خوش خبری.

No news is good news.

بیسواد کور است.

There is no blindness like ignorance.
*An illiterate is blind.*

بیکار نمی توان نشستن.

Labor as long lived.
*One cannot sit idle.*

بیگانه اگر وفا کند خویش من است.

A good friend is my nearest relation.
*A stranger is faithful; he is my relative.*

بی گدار به آب زدن.

Don't go near the water until you learn how to swim.
*To venture into the river without a ford.*

بی گناه تا پای دار میرود، اما بالای دار نمی رود.

Though the sword of justice is sharp, it will not slay the innocent.
*The innocent may go to the gallows, but will not be hanged.*

بی مایه فطیر است.

Nothing comes of nothing.
*Without yeast the bread will be unleavened.*

به مرگ می گیرد که به تب راضی شود.

Seek mickle, and get something, seek little and get nothing.
*Threaten him with death so that he may be content with fever.*

48

به هر کس هر چه قسمت بود دادند.

Every man should take his own.
*Each received whatever was his fate.*

**پا تو کفش کسی کردن.**

Poke one's nose into another man's affairs.
*To put your feet in someone else's shoes.*

**پا فشردی بردی.**

Perseverance overcomes all things.

**پا در هوا حرف زدن.**

Not to have a leg to stand on.
*To talk with one's feet in the air.*

**پارسال دوست، امسال آشنا.**

Long time, no see.
*Last year a friend, this year an acquaintance.*

**پایان شب سیه، سپید است.**

The darkest hour is just before the dawn.
*At the end of the dark night, is light.*

**پایت را به اندازهٔ گلیمت دراز کن.**

Stretch your legs according to the length of your coverlet.
*Stretch your legs according to the length of your kilim.*

پرسان، پرسان به کعبه بتوان رفت.

Seek and you shall find.
*By asking you can go to Mecca.*[*]

49

پرسیدن عیب نیست ندانستن عیب است.

He that nothing questions, nothing learns.
*Asking is not a fault, ignorance is.*

پز عالی جیب خالی.

Great boast, small roast.
*An excellent appearance, an empty pocket.*

پشت سر مرده نباید بد گفت.

Never speak ill of the dead.

پشه چو پر شد بزند پیل را.

Union makes strength.
*Gnats, in great number can beat an elephant.*

---

[*] Mecca, the holy pilgrimage city of Muslims, isin Saudi Arabia.

پشیمانی سودی ندارد.

Repentance comes too late.
*There is no use in repentance.*

پنبه در گوش گذاشتن.

To turn a deaf ear.
*To put cotton in one's ear.*

پندار نیک، کردار نیک، گفتار نیک.

See no evil, hear no evil, speak no evil.
*Good thoughts, good deeds, good words.*

50

پنهان کاری دلیل عیب است.

Wherever there is a secret, there must be something wrong.
*Covering up indicates a fault.*

پوست خرس نزده را مفروش!

Don't sell the skin till you have caught the bear.

**پول بدست آوردن آسان است، اما نگهداریش دشوار.**

Money burns a hole in someone's pocket.
*Money is easy to make, but difficult to keep.*

**پول پول را پیدا میکند و آب گودال را.**

It takes money to make money.
*Money finds money, water finds the puddle.*

**پول حرام بهای شراب شور و روسپی کور است.**

Ill gotten, ill spent.
*Money unlawfully gained is spent on sour wine and a blind whore.*

51

**پول حلّال مشکلات است.**

Money is power.
*Money solves problems.*

**پول خوشبختی نمی آورد.**

Money cannot buy happiness.
*Money does not bring happiness.*

پولداران را کباب، بی پولان دودکباب.

Those that have marbles may play, but those that have none must look on.
*For those with money, barbecue. For those without, the smoke.*

52

پول را بار خر هم می کنند.

An ass is but an ass, though laden with gold.
*Even an ass could be loaded with money.*

پول زیادی مایهٔ درد سر است.

Too much money causes trouble.

پولش از پارو بالا میره.

He is rolling in money.
*He has to shovel his money.*

پول گرد و بازار دراز.

Money is round, and rolls away.
*Money is round and the bazaar is long.*

پهلوان از پر فنی به زمین می خورد.

Good swimmers are oftenest drowned.
*The champion goes down because of excessive skill.*

پیر را به خر خریدن و جوان را به زن گرفتن نفرست.

In choosing a wife, and buying a sword, we ought not trust
another.
*Don't send an old man to buy a donkey, nor a young man to
woo a wife.*

53

پیری است و هزار درد سر.

Old age is sickness of itself.
*Old age is a thousand headaches.*

پیش چشمت داشتی شیشه کبود
زآن سـبب عالم کبـودت مینمود

To look at the world through rose colored glasses.
*You wore dark glasses and you saw the world as dark.*

پیش لوطی و معلق!

Old foxes want no tutors.
*Somersault in front of a buffoon!*

پیش رو خاله، پشت سر چاله.

Many kiss the hand they wish cut off.
*Aunt in your face, ditch digger in your back.*

پیوند زن با طلا ناگسستنی است.

Diamonds are a girl's best friend.
*The attachment of woman to gold is unbreakable.*

پیه زیادی را به پاشنه می مالند.

Abundance of things engenders disdain.
*Men who have too much tallow use it to rub on their heels.*

54

تا تنور گرم است باید نان را چسباند.

Make hay while the sun shines.
*Put the bread in the oven while it's hot.*

تا پریشان نشود کار به سامان نرسد.

When things are at worst they will mend.

تا چاه خشک نشود قدر آب ندانیم.

Health is not valued until sickness comes.
*Water is not valued until the well is dry.*

تا رنج تحمل نکنی گنج نبینی.

Without diligence, no prize.
*Without suffering, no treasure.*

تا ریشه در آب است امید ثمری هست.

While there's life, there's hope.
*As long as the root is in water, there is hope for fruit.*

تازه اول چلچلیش است.

Life begins at forty.

تازی را به زور به شکار نتوان برد.

You can lead a horse to water, but you can't make him drink.
*A hound cannot be forced to hunt.*

تا سه نشه بازی نشه.

The third time's the charm.

تافته جدا بافته.

A cut above.
*A taffeta woven separately.*

55

تا فردا خدا بزرگ است.

Let the morn come, and the meat with it.
*Until tomorrow, God is great.*

تا گوساله گاو شود دل صاحبش آب شود.

Children when they are little make their parents fools, when they are great they make them mad.
*By the time the calf becomes a cow, the farmer has given up hope.*

تا مـرد سخن نگفته بـاشد

عیب و هنرش نهفته باشد

Fools are wise as long as silent.
*Until a man speaks, his faults and talents remain hidden.*

56

تا نباشد چوب تر فرمان نبرد گاو و خر.

It is the raised stick that makes the dog obey.

تا نباشد چیزکی، مردم نگویند چیزها.

What everybody says must be true.
*Unless there is something, people would not speak.*

تا نپرسی ندانی.

He that nothing questions, nothing learns.

تا نمیرد یکی به ناکامـی

دیـگری شادکام ننشیند

One man's breath, another's death.
*Until one dies from failure, another will not see success.*

تب تند زود عرق میکند.

Hot love is soon cold.

57

ترک عادت موجب مرض است.

Old habits die hard.

ترسو همیشه سالم است.

Fear keeps a man out of danger.
*A coward always survives.*

تره به تخمش میره، حسنی به باباش.

Like father, like son.
*Leek takes after its seed, little Hassan* after his dad.*

---

* A boy's name.

تخم مرغ دزد شتر دزد میشود.

He that will steal an egg will steal an ox.
*The egg thief will be a camel thief.*

58

تشخیص درد نیمی از درمان است.

A disease known is half cured.

تعریف از خود کردن، پنبه جاویدن است.

A man's praise stinks in his own mouth.
*Self praise is like chewing cotton wool.*

تعریف زیاده بد تر از دشنام است.

Too much praise is a burden.
*Too much praise is worse than cursing.*

تکبر به خاک اندر اندازدت.

Pride goes before destruction.
*Pride will throw you down to the ground.*

تُف سر بالا به ریش صاحبش بر می گردد.

An arrow shot upright falls on the shooter's head.
*He who spits up in the air will get it back on his beard.*

تنبل نرو به سایه، سایه خودش میایه.

A lazy sheep thinks its wool heavy.
*Lazy one! "Don't go to the shade, it will come to you."*

59

توانا بود هرکه دانا بود.

Knowledge is power.
*A learned man is a powerful man.*

تو اول بگو با کیــان زیستـــی
پس آنگه بگویم که تو کیستی

Tell me with whom thou goest, and I'll tell thee what thou doest.

توبۀ گرگ مرگ است.

The death of the wolves is the safety of the sheep.
*A repentant wolf is a dead wolf.*

توبه فرمایان چرا خود توبه کمتر میکنند.

Do as the priest says, not as he does.

60

تو قدر آب چه دانی که در کنار فُراتی.

You never miss the water till the well runs dry.
*How could you know the value of water when you are beside the Euphrates.*

تو کز محنت دیگران بی غمی

نشایـد که نامت نهنـــد آدمی

Rejoice not in other's sorrow.
*You don't deserve to be called a human, if you don't get upset at other's sorrows.*

تو که بر بام خود آئیـنه داری

چرا بر بام مردم میزنی سنگ

People who live in glass houses should not throw stones.
*You who have a mirror on your roof , why do you throw stones at the neighbors roof?*

تو که روضه بلدی چرا برای خودت نمیخونی.

A bachelor's wife and maid's children are well taught.
*If you know how to preach, then preach for yourself.*

تو که لالایی میدونی چرا خوابت نمیبره.

Physician, heal thyself.
*If you know how to sing a lullaby, why don't you get to sleep?*

تو که لشگرت نبود جنگت چه بود.

Kindle not a fire that you cannot extinguish.
*Without an army why did you start war?*

61

تو نیکی میکن و در دجله انـداز

که ایـــزد در بیـــابانت دهد باز

What goes around comes around.
*Do good and throw it in the Tigris\* and God will repay you in
the desert.*

---

\* The Tigris is one of the major rivers of the Middle East.

**تیر را در چشم خودش نمی بیند، خار را در چشم دیگران می بیند.**

You can see a mote in another's eye but cannot see a beam in your own.
*He cannot see the ax in his own eyes, but sees the thorn in others.*

62

**تیری در تاریکی انداختن.**

Leap in the dark.
*An arrow shot in the dark.*

**تیشه به ریشه خود زدن.**

Don't cut the bough you're standing on.
*Taking an ax to your own root.*

جاده دزد زده تا چهل روز امن است.

Lightening never strikes twice in the same place.
*A road that has been attacked by bandits is safe for forty days.*

جایی که کچل است اسم طاس را نمیشود برد.

Name not a rope, in his house that hanged himself.
*You can't say "bald" in presence of a bald.*

جایی بنشین که برنخیزانندت.

Sit in your place and no one can make you rise.
*Sit where no one can make you rise.*

جواب ابلهان خاموشی است.

For mad words, deaf ears.
*Silence is the answer to fools.*

جوجه را آخر پائیز می شمرند.

Don't count your chickens before they're hatched.
*Chickens are counted at the end of fall.*

جون به عزرائیل نمیده.

You can't get blood out of a turnip.
*He won't give his life to Azrael (the angel of death).*

جهان چون خط و خال و چشـــم و ابروست
که هر چیزی به جای خـــویـــش نیـــکوست

There is a time and place for everything.
*Each thing is good in its own place.*

جهاندیده بسیار گوید دروغ.

A traveler may lie with authority.
*He who has seen the world, lies a lot.*

63

جهنم به آن گرمی هم که می گویند نیست.

The lion is not as fierce as he is painted.
*Hell is not as hot as they say.*

چاقو دستهٔ خودش را نمی برد.

No man fouls his hands in his own business.
*The knife does not cut its own handle.*

چاه مکن بهر کسی، اول خودت دوم کسی.

He who digs a pit for another falls in himself.

چرا آدم روزهٔ شک دار بگیرد.

When in doubt do naught.
*When you are in doubt don't fast.*

چرا عاقل کند کاری که باز آرد پشیمانی.

Better safe than sorry.
*A wise man will not do something that he will regret later.*

چراغی که به خانه رواست به مسجد حرام ا ست.

Charity begins at home.
*The light which could be used at home is forbidden to be donated to the mosque.*

چشمش هزار کار میکند که ابروش خبر ندارد.

His right hand does things that his left hand does not know about.
*His eyes do thousand things that his eyebrows don't know about.*

چشم مور و پای مار و نان ملا کس ندید.

Three things are insatiable: priests, monks, and the sea.
*No one has ever seen the eye of an ant, the feet of a snake, or the charity of a mullah.*

64

چغندر گوشت نشود، دشمن دوست نشود.

Keep yourself from a reconciled enemy.
*Beet will not become meat, an enemy will not become a friend.*

چوب به مرده زدن.

There is no use beating a dead horse.
*It is like flogging a corpse.*

چوب خدا صدا نداره، وقتی بزنه دوا نداره.

God stays long, but strikes at last.
*God's stick is noiseless but when it strikes there is no cure.*

چو بد آیـد هرچه آیـد بد شود

یک بلا ده گردد و ده صد شــود

Misfortune never comes singly.
*When bad things happen, everything else gets bad, each
calamity becomes ten, and ten becomes a hundred.*

چوب را که برداری گربه دزده حساب کارشو میکنه.

He who commits a fault thinks everyone speaks of it.
*When you raise the stick the thieving cat will flee.*

چو بد کردی مباش ایـمن ز آفات

که واجب شد طبیعت را مکافـات

Like fault, like punishment.
*When you do evil expect evil, as punishment is inevitable in the
world.*

65

چو به گشتی طبیب از خود میازار

که بیــماری توان بودن دگــر بار

Honor a physician before thou hast need of him.
*Upset not your physician after recovery, you might fall ill again.*

چو نام سگ بری چوبی به دست آر.

Talk of the devil and he will appear.
*When you mention "dog" you should get a stick.*

چو تیر از کمان رفت نآید به شست.

An occasion lost cannot be redeemed.
*An arrow once shot will not return to the hand.*

چو دخلت نیست خرج آهسته تر کن.

Never spend the money before you have it.
*If you don't have enough money, spend a little less.*

66

چو در بسته باشد چه داند کسـی

که گوهر فروش است یا پیـله ور

In sleep, what difference is there between Solomon and a fool?
*Who knows who's behind a shut door: a jeweler or a peddler.*

چــو دی رفــت و فــردا نیامد به دست

حساب از همین یک نفس کن که هست

There is no time like the present.
*Yesterday is gone and tomorrow has not come yet, so enjoy the present while it lasts.*

چو عضوی به درد آورد روزگــار

دگــر عضــوها را نــمانـد قــرار

When the head aches, all the body is the worse.
*An organ in pain will not let the body rest.*

67

چو فردا شود فکر فردا کنیم.

We will cross that bridge when we get to it.
*We think of tomorrow, when tomorrow comes.*

چون اسب نماند برنهم زین بر خران.

Who has no horse may ride on a staff.
*When there are no horses around, saddle the donkeys.*

چه برای کر بزنی، چه برای کور برقصی.

A nod is as good as a wink to a blind horse.
*Like playing music for the deaf or dancing for the blind.*

چه علی خواجه، چه خواجه علی.

Six of one, a half a dozen of the other.

68

چیزی که نپرسند تو از پیش مگوی.

Speak when you're spoken to.
*Don't say anything when you haven't been asked.*

چه خوش باشد به دل یار نخستین.

No love like the first love.
*The first love is the sweetest in one's heart.*

چه به من گو، چه به در گو چه به خر گو!

Were as good tell it to the post.
*It's the same talking to me, talking to the door, or talking to the donkey.*

حاجت مشاطه نیست حسن خدا داده را.

A good face needs no band, and a bad one deserves none.
*A God given beauty needs no beautician.*

حاجی، حاجی مکه!

Long time, no see.

حالا کجایش را دیدی!

You've ain't see nothing yet!
*What of it have you seen!*

حجب ز اندازه فزون تر بد است.

Though modesty be a virtue, yet bashfulness is a vice.
*Excessive bashfulness is no good.*

69

حرام خوری آنهم شلغم!

As well be hanged for a sheep as for a lamb.
*Why commit a theft for just a turnip.*

حرف پیشکی مایه شیشکی است.

If the sky falls, we shall catch larks.
*Foretelling can bring mockery.*

حرف حرف میاره.

One word leads to another.

حرف حق تلخ است.

Truth hurts.
*Truth is bitter.*

حرف خـودت را کجا شنیدی؟ آنجا که حرف مردم را شنیدی.

What is told in the ear of a man is often heard a 100 miles away.
*Where did you hear your own words? Where you heard other's.*

حرف راست را باید از زبان بچه شنید.

Children and fools do not lie.
*Truth must be heard from children.*

حریف، حریف خود را می شناسد.

When a Greek meets Greek, then comes the tug of war.
*Opponents know each other too well.*

حساب بدینار بخشش به خروار.

A hard gathering, a wide scattering.
*Account by the dinar, give charity by the ass load.*

حساب، حساب است، کاکا برادر.

Business is business.
*An account is an account; a brother a brother.*

حساب دو دوتا چهارتاست.

To put two and two together.
*Two twos make four.*

70

حسود هرگز نیاسود.

Envy eats nothing but its own.
*The envious is never relaxed.*

حق گرفتنی است، نه دادنی.

Ask and it shall be given you.
*Right is to be taken not to be given.*

حکم بچه از حکم شاه روان تر است.

The baby is the king of the house.
*A child's order is stronger than the king's.*

حکیمی که خود باشدش زرد روی
از او داروی سُرخرویی مجـــوی

Physician, heal thyself.
*Seek not rosy cheeks from the pale faced physician.*

حماقت هم خوب چیزیست.

Where ignorance is bliss, it's folly to be wise.
*Stupidity is a good thing.*

حوضی که آب نداره ماهی گلخار نمیخاد.

Gut no fish, till you catch them.
*A pond with no water does not need goldfish.*

71

خاله ام اگر ریش داشت دائیم می شد.

If my aunt had been a man, she'd have been my uncle.
*If my aunt had a beard she would have been my uncle.*

خانه ای را که دو کدبانوست، خاک تا زانوست.

Too many pilots wreck the ship.
*In a house with two housewives, dust is heaped up to the knees.*

خدا جامه میدهد، کو اندام؟ نان میدهد، کو دندان؟

God sends nuts to those who have no teeth.
*Gods send clothes to those with no proper figure, and bread to those with no teeth.*

خدا خر را شناخت شاخش نداد.

God sends crust cow short horns.
*God knew the ass and didn't give him horns.*

خدا روزی رسان است.

Spend, and God will send; spare and be ever bare.
*God is giver of daily bread.*

خدا سرما را بقدر بالاپوش می دهد.

God sends cold after clothes.

خدا کَس بیکَسان است.

The nest of the blind is made by God.
*God is the kin of those without kin.*

72

خداگر ز حکــمت ببندد دری

ز رحــمت گشایــد در دیگری

If God closes a door, he opens a window.

خدا نجار نیست اما در و تخته را خوب به هم می اندازد.

Every Jack has his Jill.
*God is not a carpenter, but can well match the door and frame.*

خدا نصیب گرگ بیابون نکند.

I would not wish it on my worst enemy.
*I wouldn't wish it on a savage wolf.*

خداوندا سه درد آمـد بـه یکبار

خر لنگ و زن زشت و طلبکـــار

Misfortune never comes singly.
*Oh God! Three mishaps at the same time: a limping donkey, an ugly wife and a debtor.*

خدا یه جو شانس بده.

An ounce of luck is worth a pound of wisdom.
*Oh God! Give me a bit of good luck.*

خر بارکش را هی بار می کنند.

A willing horse is run to death.
*The willing ass is always loaded.*

73

خربزهٔ شیرین نصیب کفتار می شود.

The worst hog often gets the best pear.
*The sweet melon falls into the hyena's lot.*

خر کریم را نعل کردن.

To grease someone's palm.
*To shoe Karim's* donkey.*

74

خرت بسته به، گرچه دزد آشنا است.

Caution is the parent of safety.
*Though you know the thief, it is better to tie your donkey.*

خرج که از کیـــــسۀ مهمان بود
حاتــم طایـــی شـدن آسان بود

It is easy to cry Yule at other men's cost.
*If the guest is paying, it is easy to become Hatam Tai.†*

خر خرابی میرساند از چشم گاو می بینند.

One does the scathe, and another has the scorn.
*The donkey does the damage and the cow is being punished.*

---

* A male Persian name.
† Hatam Tai. A generous man of legend.

خر عیسی گرش به مکه برند

چون بیـــایـــد هنوز خر باشد

If an ass goes a-traveling, he'll not come home a horse.
*If Jesus's ass were taken to Mecca, it would still be an ass when it returns.*

75

خر مهره را با دُر برابر کردن.

To take eggs for money.
*To equalize the glass bead and the jewel!*

خر هم دوبار پایش در یک چاله نمیره.

Even an ass doesn't fall in a pit twice.

خر همان خره، فقط پالونش عوض شده.

Cut off a dog's tail and he will be a dog still.
*He is the same ass, only his saddle has changed.*

خشت اول گر نهد معمار کج

تــا ثریا میرود دیـــــوار کج

No good building without a good foundation.
*If the architect sets the first brick crooked, the wall will be*
*crooked till the Pleiades.*

76

خشت بر آب زدن.

To carry water in a sieve.
*To lay bricks on water.*

خطا بر بزرگان گرفتن خطاست.

Don't teach your grandmother to suck eggs.
*It is a mistake to point out the errors of elders.*

خلاف جریان آب نمی شود شنا کرد.

It is ill striving against the stream.
*You can't swim against the stream.*

خلایق هرچه لایق.

You get what you deserve.

خـــلق را تقلیـــدشـــان بر باد داد

ای دو صد لعنت بر ایـن تقلیـد باد

A wise man makes his own decision, an ignorant man follows public opinion.
*Imitating can ruin people; two hundred curses upon such imitation.*

77

خواب، برادر مرگه.

Sleep is the brother of death.

خواب، خواب میاره.

One slumber finds another.

خواب دیدی خیر باشه.

Wishful thinking.
*You seem to have had a pleasant dream.*

خواب نوشین بامداد رحـیل

باز دارد پیـــــاده را ز سبیل

Who rises late must trot all day.
*Sleeping thoughtlessly at dawn of departure slows the traveler.*

خوابیده پارس میکند.

Barking dogs seldom bite.
*He barks while lying down.*

خواستن توانستن است.

Where there is a will, there is a way.
*If you wish to do, you can do it.*

خواهی نشوی رسوا همرنگ جماعت شو.

When in Rome, do as the Romans do.
*If you don't want to be disgraced, do as others do.*

78

خواهی عزیز شوی یا گور شو یا دور شو.

Familiarity breeds contempt.
*If you want to be endeared, either die or go far away.*

خوب رخی هر چه کنی کرده ای.

A good face is a letter of recommendation.
*If you're beautiful, whatever you do is fine.*

خود را به آب و آتش زدن.

To leave no stone unturned.
*To expose oneself to fire and water.*

79

خودم کردم که لعنت بر خودم باد.

Man is his own worst enemy.
*Damn me, as I did it to myself.*

خود را به جای دیگری گذاشتن.

Walking in someone else's shoes.
*To put yourself in someone else's place.*

خود گویی و خود خندی، عجب مرد هنرمندی!

Fools laugh at their own sport.
*You are an ingenious, you say and you laugh at it yourself.*

خوردن برای زیستن و ذکر کردنست

تو معتقد که زیستن از بهر خوردنست

Eat to live, not live to eat.
*One should eat in order to live and praise God; but you believe that one lives to eat!*

خوشا آن که کُره خر آمد الاغ رفت.

Ignorance is bliss.
*Happy is he who came as an ass and died as a mule.*

خوشبخت آنکه خورد و کشت و بدبخت آنکه مرد و هشت.

There was a wife that kept her supper for her breakfast,
and she died the next day.
*Happy is the one who planted and ate;*
*unfortunate is the one who gathered and left behind.*

خوش زبان باش، در امان باش.

A good tongue is a good weapon.
*A pleasant tongue keeps you safe.*

خون خون را می شوید.

Blood will have blood.

خیال میکنه از دماغ فیل افتاده.

He is a proud toad that will not scrape his own hole.
*He thinks he has been dropped out of an elephant's trunk.*

خیرش به هیچکس نمیرسد.

It is an ill wind that blows nobody any good.
*His goodness goes to no one.*

خیلی از خودش متشکر است.

He is a proud horse that will not bear his own provender.
*He is very happy with himself.*

**دادند دو گـوش و یـک زبـانت زآغاز**

**یعنی که دو بشنو و یکی بیش مـگوی**

Hear twice before you speak once.
*You were given two ears and one tongue.*
*In order to hear two words and say only one.*

**دارندگی است و برازندگی.**

They that have got a good store of butter may lay it thick on
their bread.
*The wealthy can afford to be elegant.*

**داروی کژدم زده، کشته کژدم بود.**

Like, cures like.
*The cure for someone who has bitten by scorpion is a dead*
*scorpion.*

**داشتم داشتم حساب نیست، دارم، دارم حسابست.**

Better say "here it is," than "here it was."
*It is what you have that counts, not what you used to have.*

**دانا با اشارهٔ ابرو کار کند و نادان بزخم چوگان.**

A nod for the wise, a rod for the fool.

دانا هم داند و هم پرسد، نادان نه داند و نه پرسد.

While the discreet advise, the fool does his business.
*A wise man knows and asks, while an ignorant person does not know and does not ask.*

دختر به تو میگم، عروس تو بشنو. (به در میگم که دیوار بشنود.)

I beat him to frighten you.
*I am talking to you, daughter, daughter-in law please listen.*

دختری را که مادرش تعریف کنه برای آقا دائیش خوبه!

It is not as your mother says, but as your neighbors say.
*She who is praised by her mother is only fit to be married to her uncle.*

در برابر چو گـوسفند سلیــم
در قفا همچو گرگ مردمخوار

Better an open enemy than a false friend.
*A meek sheep in your presence,*
*like a man-devouring wolf behind your back.*

در پس هر گریه آخر خنده است.

He that sings on Friday will weep on Sunday.
*After any crying, there will be laughter.*

در حوضی که ماهی نیست قورباغه سپهسالار است.

He is a triton among the minnows.
*In a pool with no fish, the frog is the commander of the army.*

در خانه ات را ببند، همسایه را دزد نکن.

Better lock than doubt.
*Lock your door and make not your neighbor a thief.*

81

درختی که تلخست ویرا سرشت

گرش بر نشانـــی به باغ بهشت

ســـرانجام کــو بر به بار آورد

همــان میـــــوه تلــخ بار آورد

No good apple on a sour stock.
*A tree which is bitter in nature will bear a bitter fruit even if
planted in the Garden of Eden.*

درخت کاهلی بارش گرسنگی است.

Idleness is the key of beggary.
*The fruit of idleness tree is hunger.*

82

درخت هرچه پربارتر، سر بزیرتر.

The more noble, the more humble.
*The more a tree is laden with fruit, the more it leans.*

درد باید باشد تا درمان باشد.

No pain, no cure.
*There should be pain, till there will be cure.*

درد کوه کوه می آید و مو مو میرود.

Sickness arrives on horseback but departs on foot.
*Pain comes in like a mountain, but leaves hair by hair.*

در دروازه را میشود بست، در دهن مردم را نمی شود.

A jar's mouth may be stopped, a man's cannot.
*One can shut the town gate, but not people's mouths.*

در شهر کوران یک چشمی پادشاه است.

In the country of the blind, the one-eyed man is king.

در شهر نی سواران باید سوار نی شد.

One must howl with the wolves.
*In the town of bamboo-riders, one must ride on bamboo.*

در عفولذتی است که در انتقام نیست.

The noblest vengeance is to forgive.
*There is a joy in forgiveness that there is not in revenge.*

در قضاوت عجله نباید کرد.

Don't judge a book by its cover.
*Don't rush to judge.*

83

در نومیدی بسی امید است
پایان شب سیه سپید است

The darkest hour is just before the dawn.
*At the end of a dark night there is light.*

دروغ مالیات ندارد.

Talking pays no toll.
*Lies have no tax.*

84

در مثل مناقشه نیست.

There is no disputing the proverbs, a fool, and the truth.
*There is no disputing over proverbs.*

دروغ مصلحت آمیز به از راست فتنه انگیز.

Better a lie that heals, than a truth that hurts.

در همیشه بروی یک پاشنه نمی چرخد.

No sun lasts a whole day.
*The door will not always turn on the same hinge.*

دست بالای دست بسیار است.

A fox knows much, but more he who catches him.
*There are many hands above your hands.*

دزد به دزد میزند.

One thief robs another.

دزد که به دزد می رسد چماقش را میزند پشت کمرش.

There is honor among thieves.
*When a thief meets another he hides his stick behind him.*

دزد بازار آشفته می خواهد.

It is good fishing in troubled water.
*Thieves like a chaotic market.*

دست پیش میگیره که پس نیفته.

The best defense is offense.

دست در کاسه و مشت در پیشانی.

Don't bite the hand that feeds you.
*Having one's hand in the bowl and one's fist at his forehead.*

85

دستش نمک ندارد.

Save a stranger from the sea, and he'll turn your enemy.
*His hands have no salt.*

دست شیطون را از پشت بسته.

He knows one point more than the devil.
*He has tied the devil's hand from behind.*

86

دست همان دست است. فقط دستکشش عوض شده.

Poison is poison, though it comes in a golden cup.
*It is the same hand, only the gloves have changed.*

دستی را که به دندان نتوان برد، ببوس.

If you cannot bite, never show your teeth.
*When you cannot bite a hand kiss it.*

دشمن نتوان حقیر و بیچاره شمرد.

There is no little enemy.
*Never count the enemy as poor and weak.*

دعوای توی خانه را نباید سر کوچه برد.

Don't wash your dirty linen in public.
*One should not take a domestic quarrel into the street.*

دل بی غم در این عالم نباشد.

No day passes without some grief.
*In this world there is no heart without sorrow.*

دلم سیر شد، اما چشمم سیر نشد.

Your eyes are bigger than your stomach.
*My stomach is full, but not my eyes.*

دَم غنیمت است.

No time like the present.
*Let's make the best of the moment.*

دندان اسب پیش کشی را نمی شمرند.

Never look a gift horse in the mouth.
*One does not count the teeth of a gift horse.*

87

دندانی را که درد میکند باید کشید.

Better to have it out than be always aching.
*A tooth that is aching must be pulled.*

دنیا دار مکافات است.

As a man sows, so shall he reap.
*There is comeuppance in this world.*

دنیا به کام ابلهان است.

Fools have the best luck.
*The world is to the satisfaction of fools.*

دنیا جای آزمایش است نه آسایش.

Life is a battle not a feast.
*The world is where you are tested, not rested.*

دنیا را چه دیدی.

You never know your luck.
*What have you seen from the world?*

88

دنیا را هرطور بگیری می گذرد.

Take it easy.
*Life will pass by, how ever you live it.*

دو بار با طناب کسی به چاه افتادن.

It is a silly fish that is caught twice with the same bait.
*To fall in the well twice because of the same rope.*

89

دودش به چشم خودت می رود.

As you bake, so shall you eat.
*The smoke will hurt your own eyes.*

دوری و دوستی.

Absence makes the heart grow fonder.
*Distance and friendship.*

دوست آن باشد که گیرد دست دوست در پریشانحالی و درماندگی.

A friend in need is a friend indeed.
*A friend holds a friend's hand in need.*

دوست آنست کو معایب دوست همچو آینه روبرو گوید.

He is a good friend that speaks well of me behind my back.
*A real friend is like a looking-glass who reflects your faults.*

دوست را چیست به ز دیدن دوست.

It is merry when friends meet.
*What is better for a friend than seeing a friend.*

90

دوست مرا یاد کند ولو به یک هِل پوچ.

He who gives me small gifts would have me live.
*Let friends remember me even if by a trifle.*

دوست مشمار آنکه در نعمت زند

لاف یاری وبرادرخواندگــــــی

Rich folks have many friends.
*He is not a friend who is only around at the time of prosperity.*

دوستی را هزار کس شـــاید

دشمنی را یکی بود بسیـــار

One enemy is too many, a hundred friends too few.
*A thousand friends are acceptable, one enemy is too many.*

دوستی دوستی از سرت می کنند پوستی.

God defend me from my friends; from my enemies I can
defend myself.
*In the guise of friendship they take your skin off.*

91

دوست نباید ز دوست در گله باشد.

Love your friend with his fault.
*Friends should not take offense at each other's acts.*

دوست وفادار بهتر از خویش است.

A good friend is my nearest relation.
*A loyal friend is better than a relative.*

دوست همه کس دوست هیچکس نیست.

A friend to everybody is a friend to nobody.

دو صد گفته چون نیم کردار نیست.

Action speaks louder than words.
*Two hundred words are not as good as half a deed.*

دو کس رنج بیهوده بردند و سعی بیفایده کردند، یکی آنکه اندوخت و نخورد،
دیگر آنکه آموخت و نکرد.

A good man that keeps riches and enjoys them not is like an ass that carries gold and eats thistles.

*Two types of people toiled in vain; those who gathered money but enjoyed it not, and those who learned but practiced it not.*

92

دولت جاوید یافت آنکه نکونام زیست.

A good name is better than riches.
*He who has a good name enjoyed everlasting riches.*

دولت همه ز اتفاق خیزد، بی دولتی از نفاق خیزد.

United we stand, divided we fall.
*Wealth comes from being united, poverty from being divided.*

دو نفـر دزد خـــری دزدیـدند

سر تقسیــم به هـم جنگیـدند

آندو بودند چو گرم زد و خورد

دزد سـوم خـــرشان را زد و برد

Two dogs strive with a bone, and a third runs away with it.
*Two thieves stole an ass; while they were fighting over it a third thief stole it from them.*

93

ده درویش در گلیمی بخُسبند و دو پادشاه در اقلیمی نگنجند.

Two suns cannot shine in one sphere.
*Ten dervishes may sleep on a kilim but two kings cannot rule one land.*

دهن سگ به لقمه دوخته به.

Cast a bone in the devil's teeth, and he'll save you.
*Better to stop the dog's mouth with a morsel.*

دهنش چاک و بست ندارد.

He has a loose tongue.
*There is no shutting his mouth.*

دیر بجنبی ول معطلی.

You snooze, you lose.

94

دیگ به دیگ میگه روت سیاه.

Pot calling the kettle black.
*The pot calls another pot the black face.*

دیگران کاشتند و ما خوردیم، ما بکاریم دیگران بخورند.

Walnuts and pears you plant for your heirs.
*Others planted and we ate. We should plant, so others may eat.*

دیگ شراکت به جوش نیاید.

A pot that belongs to many is ill stirred and worse boiled.
*A jointly owned pot does not boil.*

دیوار موش داره، موش هم گوش داره.

Walls have ears.
*The walls have mice, and mice have ears.*

دیوانه چو دیوانه ببیند خوشش آید.

An ass is most pleasing to another ass.
*The fool is pleased to see another fool.*

ر

رسید مژده که ایام غم نخواهد ماند

چنان نماند و چنین نیز نخواهد ماند

Cloudy mornings turn to clear evenings.
*The news has arrived that the time for sorrow is over.*
*It has not always been so and it will not remain this way.*

رطب خورده منع رطب چون کند.

Practice what you preach.
*How can the eater of dates forbid the eating of dates.*

رنج چو عادت شود آسودگیست.

It is nothing when you're used to it.
*Suffering becomes comfort when you get used to it.*

رنگ رخساره خبر می دهد از سرّ ضمیر.

The joy of the heart makes the face fair.
*The color of the face can reveal the inner secret.*

روز از نو، روزیِ از نو.

Another day, another dollar.
*A new day, a new earning.*

روزی گربه دست زن شلخته است.

Cats eat what hussies spare.

95

روکه نیست سنگ پای قزوین است.

He has got a lot of gall.

ریاضت کش به بادامی بسازد

دل عـاشـق به پیــغامی بسازد

He has enough who is contented with little.
*The lover is happy with just a message from his sweet heart.*

روضه نخونده گریه میکنه.

Don't cry before you're hurt.
*He cries before hearing the sermon.*

روی زیبا مرهم دلهای خسته است و کلید درهای بسته.

Beauty opens all doors.
*A beautiful face soothes tired hearts and opens closed doors.*

رهرو آنست که آهسته و پیوسته رود.

Slow and steady wins the race.
*The true wayfarer is the one who goes slowly and steadily.*

ریش و قیچی هر دو دست شماست.

He who has the frying-pan in his hand turns it at will.
*The beard and the scissors are both in your hands.*

ریگ به کفش داشتن.

To have something up one's sleeve.
*To have pebble in one's shoes.*

96

زاهدان کاین جلوه در محراب و منبر می کنند

چون به خلوت میروند آن کار دیگر می کنند

Do on the hill as you would do in the hall.
*Some preachers of piety do otherwise in private.*

زبان بریـده به کنجی نشسته صُم بُکم

به از کسی که نباشد زبانش انـدر حکم

Don't talk unless you can improve on silence.
*Better to be dumb than to have a tongue which is not under control.*

زبان در دهان پاسبان سر است.

Death and life are in the power of the tongue.
*The tongue is a watchman for the head.*

زبان سرخ سر سبز می دهد بر باد.

The tongue talks at the head's cost.
*The red tongue can have your head cut off.*

زبان مردم تازیانه خداست.

The voice of the people, the voice of God.
*The people's tongue is the scourge of God.*

ز تعارف کم کن و بر مبلغ افزا.

Less of your courtesy and more of your money.

زخم به گردد ولی ماند نشانش سالها.

The wound may be healed, yet a scar remains.

زخم زبان از زخم شمشیر بدتر است.

The tongue is like a sharp knife, it kills without drawing blood.
*The tongue strikes worse than a sword.*

97

ز دست دیده و دل هـــر دو فریاد

که هرچه دیده بیـند، دل کند یاد

What the eye does not see, the heart does not grieve.
*Heaven save us from the eye and the heart, for whatever the
eye sees the heart desires.*

زرنگی زیاد مایۀ جوانمرگی است.

Too much cunning undoes.
*Too much cunning brings untimely death.*

زر بر سر پولاد نهی نرم شود.

Gold will even soften steel.

98

ز گهواره تا گور دانش بجوی.

Even if we study to old age we shall not finish learning.
*Keep on learning from the cradle to the grave.*

زمان به عقب بر نمی گردد.

One cannot turn back the clock.

زمانه با تو نسازد، تو با زمانه بساز.

If life hands you lemon, make lemonade.
*If destiny does not fit you, fit yourself to destiny.*

زمین شوره سنبل برنیـــــارد
در او تخــم عمل ضایع مگردان

Of a thorn springs not a fig.
*Hyacinth will not grow in brackish soil; don't waste the seed in it.*

زن جوان را تیری در پهلو به که پیری.

A young maid married to an old man is like a new house
thatched with old straw.
*An arrow in the side of a young woman is better than having an
old man by her side.*

99

زن خوب و فرمانبـر پارسا

کند مرد درویش را پادشا

A good wife and health is a man's best wealth.
*A good obedient wife will make a king out of a poor man.*

زندگی هزار چرخ دارد.

Life is but a span.
*Life has a thousand turns.*

زنی که جهاز نداره اینهمه ناز نداره.

A tocherless dame, sits long at home.
*A Women who has no dowry should not be fussy.*

زورش به خر نمیرسه پالانش را می دزده.

He that cannot beat the ass, beats the saddle.
*The donkey was too strong for him, so he stole the pack-saddle.*

100

زیاد سخت نگیر.

Take it easy.
*Don't take it too hard.*

زیر اندازش زمین است و رو اندازش آسمان.

He is sky-clad.
*The earth is his rug and the sky his quilt.*

زیر کاسه نیم کاسه ای است.

There are wheels within wheels.
*There is a half-size bowl under the large one.*

زیره به کرمان می برد.

To carry coals to Newcastle.
*Taking cumin to Kerman.**

---

* The town of Kerman is famous for its cumin.

**سالی که نکوست از بهارش پیداست.**

If the beginning is good the end must be perfect.
*A good year is known by it's spring.*

**سبیل کسی را چرب کردن.**

To grease someone's palm.
*To grease someone's mustache.*

**سپلشت آید و زن زاید و میهمان عزیزت ز در آید.**

Misfortune never comes singly.
*While one has had bad luck in gambling, one's wife gives birth
to a baby, and one has to entertain a dear guest.*

**سحر خیز باش تا کامروا باشی.**

Early to bed, early to rise makes a man healthy, wealthy & wise.
*Rise early and become successful.*

**سخت میگیرد جهان بر مردمان سخت کوش.**

All work and no play makes Jack a dull boy.
*Life will be hard for those who take it hard.*

**سخن گفته و قضای رفته و تیر انداخته باز نگردد.**

A word and a stone let go cannot be called back.
*A word said, a fate befallen, and an arrow shot will not return.*

سخن هرچه گویی، همان بشنوی.

Ask a silly question; get a silly answer.

101

سر بشکند در کلاه، دست بشکند در آستین.

Don't wash your dirty linen in public.
*If one's head is broken, let it be in one's hat, and if one's arm is broken, let it be in one's sleeve.*

سرخر باش صاحب زر باش.

It is not what he is, but what he has.
*Be an ass's head, but be rich.*

سرش به تنش سنگینی میکند.

The gallows groans for him.
*He feels a heavy head on his shoulder.*

سرکه مفت از عسل شیرین تر است.

Stolen waters are sweet.
*Free vinegar is sweeter than honey.*

سر و جان به فدای شکم.

Better belly burst than good meat lost.
*I sacrifice my life for my stomach.*

102

سُر و مُر و گُنده.

Fit as a fiddle.


سُرنا را از سر گشادش زدن.

To put the cart before the horse.
*To play the oboe from the wrong end.*


سری که درد نمیکنه دستمال نمی بندند.

If it ain't broke, don't fix it.
*A handkerchief is not tied to a head which does not ache!*


سفر آدمی را پخته می کند.

Travel broadens the mind.
*Traveling matures a man.*

سفره دلش پیش همه پهن است.

To wear your heart on your sleeve.
*His heart is open to everyone.*

سکوت علامت رضاست.

Silence gives consent.
*Silence is a sign of consent.*

103

سگ به دریای هفتگانه بشوی

چونکه تـر شـد پلیدتر بـاشـد

Cut off a dog's tail and he will be a dog still.
*Wash a dog in the seven seas, it will be even fouler when it gets wet.*

سگ به قلادهٔ زرین شکار نکند.

Cat in gloves catches no mice.
*Golden collar does not make a hunter of a dog.*

سگ در حضور به از برادر دور.

A near neighbor is better than a far-dwelling kinsman.
*Better a dog that is near than a brother far off.*

سگ، سگ را نمی خورد.

There is honor among thieves.
*Dog does not eat dog.*

سگ زرد برادر شغال است.

One is as bad as the other.
*A yellow dog is the brother of the jackal.*

سگ لاید و کاروان گذرد.

The dogs bark, but the caravan goes on.

104

سگ سیر و قلیهٔ ترش.

When the mouse has had enough, the meal is bitter.
*When the dog gets full, the dish tastes sour.*

سلمانی را با سر کچل ما یاد میگیره.

A barber learns to shave by shaving fools.
*He learns cutting hair by practicing on my bald head.*

سلمانی ها وقتی بیکار میشوند سر همدیگر را می تراشند.

One barber shaves another gratis.
*Barbers, when idle, shave each other's heads.*

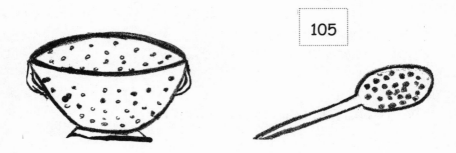

سنگ بزرگ علامت نزدن است.

He that does most at once, does least.
*Threatening with a large rock is a sign of not intending to throw.*

سنگی را که نتوان برداشت، باید بوسید و گذاشت.

If you can't beat them, join them.
*The stone which cannot be lifted should be kissed.*

سوداگر، پنیر از شیشه می خورد.

The shoemaker's son always goes barefoot.
*The miser eats cheese from the outside of the cheese container.*

سوسکه به بچه اش می گفت قربون دست و پای بلوریت برم.

The crow thinks her own birds whitest.
*The beetle says to the child: "what white limbs you have."*

سیب سرخ برای دست چلاق خوبست.

The worst hog often gets the best pear.
*The red apple is good for the cripple's hand.*

سیر از گرسنه خبر نداره.

He whose belly is full believes not in him who is fasting.
*The full stomach does not know of the hungry stomach.*

سیر یک روز طعنه زد به پیاز

که تو مسکین چقدر بد بویی

Pot calling the kettle black.
*The garlic said to the onion: "you stink."*

سیلی نقد به از حلوای نسیه.

Better an egg today than a hen tomorrow.
*A ready slap on the face is better than promised halvah.*

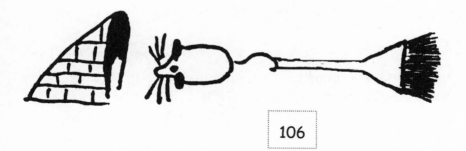

106

شادی بی غم در این بازار نیست.

Sadness and gladness succeed each other.
*There is no joy without sorrow in this bazaar.*

شانس را باید قاپید.

If heaven drops a date, open your mouth.
*Opportunity should be grabbed.*

شانس فقط یکبار در خانه آدم را می زند.

Opportunity seldom knocks twice.
*Luck knock's on one's door only once.*

شاهنامه آخرش خوش است.

Praise a fair day at night.
*It is the end of the "Shahnameh"\* that is pleasant.*

شب تاریک رفت و آمد روز.

Bad day has good night.
*The dark night went and the day came.*

---

\* "The Book of Kings," the major Persian epic poem.

شپش تنش منیژه خانم است. (آدم افاده ای)

He thinks his fart as sweet as musk.

*His louse is lady Manijeh.**

107

شتر در خـــواب بیند پنبه دانه

گهی لُف لُف خورد گه دانه دانه

The cat dreams of mice.
*The camel dreams of eating cotton seeds.*

شتر دیدی ندیدی.

You see nothing, you hear nothing.
*Remember, if you're asked, you didn't see the camel.*

شریک دزد و رفیق قافله.

You can't run with the hare and hunt with the hounds.
*A partner of the robber and a companion of the caravan.*

---

* A woman's name.

شغالی که از باغ قهر کنه، باغبون منفعت میکنه.

The death of the wolves is the safety of the sheep.
*If the jackal is not on speaking terms with the garden, the gardener profits.*

108

شکم گرسنه زبان سرش نمی شود.

Hungry bellies have no ears.
*A hungry stomach understands nothing.*

شنیدن کی بود مانند دیدن؟

Seeing is believing.
*When was hearing like seeing?*

شوی زن زشت روی نابینا به.

Blind man's wife needs no paint.
*An ugly woman's husband better be blind.*

شیشه بشکسته را پیوند کردن مشکل است.

A cracked bell can never sound well.
*It is hard to mend a broken glass.*

شیطان در لباس فرشته.

Wolf in sheep's clothing.
*The devil in angels clothing.*

شیون قبل از مرگ.

Don't cry before you're hurt.
*Mourning before death.*

109

صبر است و زر چارهٔ کارها.

Patience, time and money accommodate all things.
*Patience and money answer problems.*

صبر کن تا خرت از پل بگذرد.

Call the bear "uncle" until you're safe across the bridge.
*Wait till your ass crosses the bridge.*

صبر و ظفر هر دو دوستان قدیمند.

Patient men win the day.
*Patience and victory are old friends.*

صد بارگز کن یکبار ببر.

Think on the end before you begin.
*Measure a hundred times and cut once.*

صد تا چاقو میسازد، یکیش دسته ندارد.

Great promises and small performances.
*He makes a hundred knives none of which has a handle.*

صلاح مملکت خویش خسروان دانند.

Every man knows his own business best.
*Kings know what is best for their country.*

صنار بده آش به همین خیال باش.

Wishful thinking.

صورت زیبای ظاهر هیچ نیست

ای بـــرادر سیرت زیبا بیــار

Goodness is better than beauty.
*Outer beauty is no good, bring me inner beauty.*

110

ض

ضرر را از هر جا جلویش را بگیرند منفعت است.

Never too late to mend.
*Whenever you cut loss, it is gain.*

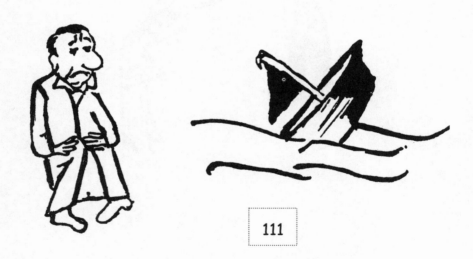

طاس اگر نیک نشیند همه کس نَراد است.

He dances well to whom fortune pipes.
*If the dice are lucky, everyone is a good backgammon player.*

طرب، افسرده کند دل چو ز حد درگذرد.

Joy surfeited turns to sorrow.
*Excessive indulgence brings sadness.*

طمع را نبایـــد که چـندان کنی

که صاحب کرم را پشیمان کنی

All covet, all lose.
*Do not be too greedy, or the giver will repent.*

طمع زیادی فقر می آورد.

Catch not at the shadow and lose the substance.*

---

* Reference to one of Aesop's fables in which a dog, carrying a bone, catches
sight of his reflection in a pond and snaps greedily at the bone reflected
there. The real bone slips out of his mouth and is lost.

ظالم همیشه خانه خرابست.

Malice hurts itself most.
*An oppressor will always end up in misery.*

ع

عادت طبیعت ثانوی است.

Habit is a second nature.

عاشق بی پول باید شبدر بچینه.

When poverty comes in at the door, love flies out of the window.
*A penniless lover should pick clover.*

عاقبت جوینده یابنده بود.

Seek and you shall find.

عاقبت خشم پشیمانی است.

Anger begins with folly, and ends with repentance.
*Anger ends with repentance.*

عاقبت خیاط در کوزه افتاد.

The biter is sometimes bit.
*In the end the tailor fell into the jar.*

---

* Refers to the story of a tailor who dropped a pebble in a jar every time someone died in his town until he died himself.

عاقبت گرگ زاده گرگ شود

گرچه با آدمــــی بزرگ شود

The wolf may lose his teeth but never his nature.
*The wolf is still a wolf, even if raised among humans.*

113

عاقل بکنار آب تا پل می جست،

دیوانه پابرهنه از آب گــذشت

Desperate times call for desperate measures.
*While the wise man was looking for the bridge, the fool crossed the river barefooted.*

عالِم بی عمل مثل درخت بی ثمر است.

A man of words and not of deeds is like a garden full of weeds.
*A learned man without deeds is like a fruitless tree.*

عجب حلال زاده ایست.

Talk of the devil, and in he walks.

عجله کار شیطان است.

Haste is the devil's work.

عدو شود سبب خیر اگر خدا خواهد.

Misfortune does not always come to injure.
*If God will it, the enemy will bring you luck.*

عروس بلد نیست برقصه میگه اطاق کجه.

A bad workman blames his tool.
*The bride does not know how to dance and says: "The room is crooked."*

عزت هرکس به دست آنکس است.

He that respects not, is not respected.
*Everyone's respect is in his own hands.*

عشق در آمد به دل، رفت ز سر عقل و هوش.

One cannot love and be wise.
*Love comes into the heart, out goes the wisdom.*

114

عسس بیا منو بگیر.

Put your finger in the fire and say it was your fortune.
*Officer! Come and arrest me.*

عشق کور است.

Love is blind.

115

عشق منطق سرش نمی شود.

Affection blinds reason.
*Love does not understand logic.*

عشق و مُشک پنهان نمی ماند.

Love, a cough, and the itch cannot be hid.
*Love and the odor of musk cannot be hidden.*

عشق یک سره مایهٔ دردسره.

Love is a two way street.
*One way love causes trouble.*

عقل سالم در بدن سالم است.

A sound mind in a sound body.

عقلش پاره سنگ برمیدارد.

He's got a screw loose.

عقل که نیست جون در عذابه.

What is not wisdom is danger.
*Lack of wisdom brings torment to the spirit.*

116

عقلی که به چهل سالگی نیاد هیچوقت نمیاد.

A fool at forty is a fool indeed.
*If wisdom does not come by forty, it will never come.*

علاج واقعه قبل از وقوع باید کرد.

An ounce of prevention is worth a pound of cure.
*The remedy should be thought of before the accident.*

علف باید به دهن بزی شیرین بیاید.

One man's meat is another man's poison.
*The grass has to be sweet to the goat's mouth.*

علم چـــندانکه بیشتر خوانی

چون عمل در تو نیست نادانی

Action is the proper fruit of knowledge.
*The more you acquire learning, so long as you do not practice it, you are ignorant.*

117

عیب می جمله بگفتی، هنرش نیز بگوی.

Give the devil his due.
*You have enumerated the evils of wine, it is fair to mention its virtues as well.*

عیسی به دین خود، موسی به دین خود.

To each his own.
*Jesus to his religion, Moses to his.*

عینک سواد نمی آورد.

It is not the beard that makes the philosopher.
*It is not the glasses that brings knowledge.*

غم آن درد که درمان نپذیرد چه خوری؟

Never grieve for what you cannot help.
*Never grieve over a pain you can't cure.*

غم خواران را غم دهید و می خواران را می.

An opium smoker will always find opium.
*Give grief to those who like to grieve and wine to those who like to drink.*

غم فردا نشاید خوردن امروز.

Let your trouble tarry till its own day come.
*Don't think of tomorrow's sorrow today.*

غنیمت دان دمی تایک دَمت هست.

No time like the present.
*make the best of every moment.*

غوره مویز میشود، ولی مویز غوره نمی شود.

Every oak has been an acorn.
*Some sour grapes become raisins, but a raisin does not become a sour grape.*

غوره نشده مویز شده.

Every spart now-a-day's calls itself a herring.
*He's hardly a sour grape, yet behaves like a raisin.*

غیبت آخوند، عید شاگردان است.

When the cat is away the mice will play.
*The teacher's absence is the student's holiday.*

فتنهٔ خفته را بیدار مکن.

Wake not a sleeping lion.

فردا را کی دیده.

Tomorrow may never come.
*No one has seen tomorrow.*

فردا هم روز خداست.

Tomorrow is another day.
*Tomorrow is also God's day.*

فرزند عزیز دردونه یا دَنگه یا دیوونه.

He that has one hog makes him fat; and he that has one son
makes him a fool.
*A spoiled child ends up either stupid or crazy.*

فضولی موقوف!

Don't stick your nose in someone else's business.

فلفل نبین چه ریزه، بشکن ببین چه تیزه.

A little body often harbor's a great soul.
*Though pepper is a tiny thing, its taste is mighty powerful.*

فواره چون بلند شود سرنگون شود.

What goes up, must come down.
*When a fountain rises it must fall.*

فیل خوابی بیند و فیلبان خوابی.

One thing thinks the horse, and another he that leads him.
*The elephant dreams of one thing, the elephant-rider of another.*

119

**قاش زین را بگیر چاک سواری پیشکشت.**

We must learn to walk before we can run.
*Hold on to the saddle before the horse starts to run.*

**قبای بعد از عید برای گل منار خوبه.**

Advice comes too late when a thing is done.
*When the new year is over, a new suit loses its value.*

**قحبهٔ پیرچه کند که توبه نکند از نابکاری.**

The devil grew sick and a monk he would be.
*What can an old harlot do but repent of her misdeeds.*

**قدر عافیت کسی داند که به مصیبتی گرفتار آید.**

Misfortunes tell us what fortune is.
*He who has suffered adversity will value good health.*

**قربان بند کیفتم تا پول داری رفیقتم.**

When good cheer is lacking, our friends will go packing.
*I'm the slave of your purse, as long as you have money I'll be your friend.*

**قطره قطره جمع گردد وانگهی دریا شود.**

Many drops make a flood.
*Drops by drops will make a sea.*

قرض به لرزش نمی ارزد.

Neither a borrower nor a lender be.
*Borrowing is not worth its fears.*

120

قلم از شمشیر برنده تر است.

The pen is mightier than the sword.

قُمپز در کردن.

They can do least who boast louder.

قناعت توانگر کند مرد را.

He is rich enough that wants nothing.
*Contentment makes men powerful and rich.*

قول مرد یکی است.

The bird is known by his note, the man by his words.
*The word of a man is one thing.*

کاچی به از هیچی.

Half a loaf is better than none.
*Kachi* is better than nothing.

کار امروز به فردا مفکن.

Never put off till tomorrow what you can do today.

کار حضرت فیل است.

It is a tough nut to crack.
*It is a job for his excellency the elephant.*

کار از کار گذشته.

The die is cast.
*What's done is done.*

کار را که کرد، آنکه تمام کرد.

Better never to begin than never to make an end.
*He who finished the job, did the job.*

کار، کار شیطان است.

The devil made me do it.
*The devil did it.*

---

کار عار نیست.

Work is no disgrace.

121

کار نشد ندارد.

Nothing is impossible to a willing heart.

کار نیکو کردن از پر کردن است.

Practice makes perfect.
*Doing good is doing it often.*

کارها آسان شود اما به صبر.

All things are difficult before they are easy.
*With patience all work becomes easy.*

کار هر بز نیست خرمن کوفتن

گاو نر مـی خواهد و مرد کهن

Only elephant can bear an elephant load.
*Harvesting is not the work of a goat,*
*an ox and a mature man are needed.*

کاسهٔ صبرم لبریز شده.

The drop makes the cup run down.
*The bowl of my patience is running over.*

کار یکبار اتفاق می افتد.

It happens in an hour, that happens not in seven years.
*It happens at once.*

کاسه داغ تر از آش.

More Catholic than the Pope.
*A bowl hotter than the soup.*

122

کاسه همسایه شکم را سیر نمی کند، محبت را زیاد می کند.

Small presents keep up friendship.
*The dish sent by a neighbor does not satisfy your hunger, but increases affection.*

کاشکی را کاشتند سبز نشد.

Pigs might fly if they had wings.
*They planted "if only." It did not grow.*

کافر همه را به کیش خود پندارد.

Who is in fault suspects everybody.
*The irreligious thinks all are irreligious.*

123

کاهلی شاگرد بدبختی است.

Idleness is the root of all evil.
*Laziness brings misery.*

کبوتر با کبـــــــوتر بـاز با باز

کند همجنس با همجنس پرواز

Birds of a feather flock together.
*Pigeon with pigeon, falcon with falcon.*

کجا خوش است آنجا که دل خوش است.

Where it is well with me, there is my country.

گُره دادن و شتر خواستن.

To throw a sprat to catch a mackerel.
*To offer a foal and ask for a camel.*

كَس نخارد پشت من جز ناخن انگشت من.

If you want a thing done, do it yourself.
*No one will scratch my back but my own finger nails.*

کس نگوید که دوغ من ترش است.

No one cries stinking fish.
*No one says, "my yogurt is sour."*

کسی از دل کسی خبر ندارد.

None knows the weight of another man's burden.
*No one knows of another's heart.*

کسی که از گرگ می ترسد، نباید گوسفند نگهدارد.

If you can't take the heat, stay out of the kitchen.
*He who is afraid of wolves, should not be a shepherd.*

124

کسی که بار شیشه دارد به دیوانه سنگ نمی زند.

Those who live in glass houses should not throw stones.
*He who is carrying glass, should not throw stones at madmen.*

کسی رایگان چیز ندهد به کسی.

You don't get something for nothing.
*No one gives anything for free to anyone.*

125

کف دست ما که مو نداره تو هم یکی ازش بکن.

He that has nothing has nothing to lose.
*My palm has no hair, pluck a hair from it.*

کفش پینه دوز پاشنه ندارد.

The cobbler's children have holes in their soles.
*The shoemaker has no heel on his shoe.*

کفگیر به ته دیگ خورده.

It is too late to spare when the bottom is bare.
*The ladle has hit the bottom of the pot.*

کک تو تنبونش افتاده.

He has ants in his pants.
*He has fleas in his pants.*

كل اگر طبیب بودی، سر خود دوا نمودی.

Physician, heal thyself.
*Were the bald man a doctor, he would cure his own baldness.*

کلاغ از باغمون قهر کرده، یک گردو به منفعت ما.

The death of the wolves is the safety of the sheep.
*When the crow stops speaking to our garden, it is a few walnuts in our favor.*

کلاغ از وقتی بچه دار شد شکم سیر به خود ندید.

He that has children, all his morsels are not his own.
*Since the crow had young ones, she has not had a full stomach.*

126

کلاغ اومد راه رفتن کبک را یاد بگیره، راه رفتن خودش هم از یادش رفت.

Every man to his trade.
*In an attempt to learn the strutting of the partridge, the crow forgot its own manner of walking.*

کلاغ سر لونۀ خودش قار قار نمیکنه.

It is an ill bird that fouls its own nest.
*The crow does not screech on his own nest.*

کلاه تقی را سر نقی گذاشتن.

To rob Peter to pay Paul.
*To put Taghi's hat on Naghi's head.*

کلبهٔ احزان شود روزی گلستان، غم مخور.

If today will not, tomorrow will.
*Your house of sorrow will become a rose garden one day.*

کم گوی و گزیده گوی چون دُرّ.

A wise head makes a closed mouth.
*Speaking little and choosing your words like pearls.*

127

کم گیری کمت گیرم، نمرده ماتمت گیرم.

Claw me and I'll claw thee.
*Take me for little and I'll take you for little,*
*I'll mourn you before your death.*

کنار گود نشسته میگه لنگش کن.

Monday morning quarterbacking.
*To sit by the ring and tell the man inside: "knock him down."*

کوری عصاکش کور دگر شود.

The blind leading the blind.
*One blind man carrying the other's walking stick.*

کور که می میرد بادامی چشم می شود.

Praise no man, until he is dead.
*When a blind man dies, he is praised as having beautiful eyes.*

کوزه گر از کوزه شکسته آب می خورد.

The cobbler's children have holes in their soles.
*The potter drinks from a broken jug.*

کوزۀ نو تا دو روز آب را سرد نگهمیدارد.

A new broom sweeps clean.
*A new jug keeps the water cool for two days.*

128

کوفته را نان تهی کوفته است.

Hunger is the best sauce.
*Dry bread is like meat ball for a run down man.*

کوه به کوه نمیرسد، آدم به آدم می رسد.

Friends may meet, but mountains never.

کهن جامهٔ خویش پیراستن

به از جامهٔ عاریت خواستن

Better spare to have of your own, than ask of other men.
*Better to mend your clothes than to borrow someone else's.*

کی؟ وقت گل نی.

When pigs fly.
*When bamboo blossoms.*

129

گاه باشد که کودکی نادان به خطا بر هدف زند تیـری.

A fool's bolt may sometimes hit the mark.
*It may happen that an unknowing knowing child might hit a target by chance.*

گاهی از دروازه بیرون نمی رود، گاهی از چشمهٔ سوزن بیرون می رود.

He strains at a gnat and swallows a camel.
*Sometimes he passes through a needle's eye, and sometimes he does not pass through the town-gate.*

گدا را چو حاصل شود نــان شام

چنان شاد خسبد که سلطان شام

Poor folks are glad of porridge.
*If a beggar finds some bread for dinner, he would sleep as happy as the king of Syria.*

گدا را نباید که باشد غرور.

Beggars can't be choosers.
*Beggars should not have pride.*

گدارا که رو بدهی صاحبخانه می شود.

Give him an inch and he'll take a yard.
*If you give the beggar too much, he will become your landlord.*

گذشته ها گذشته.

Let bygones be bygones.

130

گربه دستش به گوشت نمیرسه میگه پیف پیف چه بو میده.

The fox when he cannot reach the grapes says they are not ripe.
*The cat who can't reach the meat, says "it stinks."*

گربه شد عابد و مسلمانا.

When the fox preaches, then beware of your geese.
*The cat pretending to be a devoted Muslim.*

گربه شیـــر است در گرفتن مـوش
لیک موش است در مصـاف پلنگ

Every man is a pirate in a calm sea.
*The cat is a lion in catching a mouse, but she is a mouse when
confronted with the leopard.*

گر حکم شود کـه مست گیرند

در شـهر هر آنکه هست گیرند

Let he who is without sin cast the first stone.
*Should the order go forth to arrest the drunk, they would have to arrest the whole town.*

گر زر داری به زور محتاج نئی.

Money makes the mare go.
*If you have money you need no force.*

گرسنگی نکشیدی که عاشقی از یادت بره.

Hunger is stronger than love.
*You have not been hungry enough to forget about love.*

131

گر صبر کنی ز غوره حلوا سازی.

With time and art, the leaf of the mulberry-tree becomes satin.
*If you have patience, I'll make halvah from sour grape.*

گرگ اگر در لباس چوپان رفت

وای بر حـال گـــــوسفندان است

Set not the fox to keep the geese.
*If the wolf is dressed as a shepherd,*
*oh woe to the sheep!*

132

گرگ در لباس میش.

Wolf in sheep's clothing.

گر گفتن سیم است، خاموشی زر است.

Speech is silver, but silence is golden.

گِرهی که به دست باز میشود به دندان نباید باز کرد.

Never take a stone to break an egg when you can do it with the
back of your knife.
*A knot that can be opened by hand should not be opened by*
*teeth.*

گر هنری داری و هفتاد عیـب

دوست نبیند بجز آن یک هنر

Faults are thick where love is thin.
*If you have one virtue and seventy faults, he who loves you will*
*see nothing but the virtue.*

گز نکرده پاره کردن.

Don't go near the water until you learn how to swim.
*To cut the fabric before measuring it.*

گفت از عیب خویش بـی خبری

وانگه از خلق عیـــب می جویـــی

The camel never sees its own hump, but that of its brother is
always before its eyes.
*Unaware of your own faults, but finding faults in others.*

133

گفتند برو کلاه بیار، رفت سر آورد.

Burn not your house to frighten the mouse away.
*I asked for a hat, he brought me a head.*

گفتند پیش نیا میفتی، آنقدر پس رفت که از آن سو افتاد.

Too far east is west.
*He was told not to come forward he may fall, he went too far
back till he fell the other side.*

134

گل بی خار نمی شود.

No rose without a thorn.

گل بی عیب خداست.

Among men, who is faultless.
*The flower without flaw is God.*

گِلشون را از یک خاک برداشتند.

Chip off the old block.

گلیم بخت کسی را که بافتند سیـــــاه

به آب زمزم و کوثر سفید نتوان کرد

It is better to be born lucky than rich.
*If the rug of your luck has been woven in black,
even the water of Zamzam* cannot whiten it.*

---

\* A stream in paradise.

گنجشک امروزی به گنجشک دیروزی پریدن یاد میده.

Goslings lead the geese to water.
*The baby sparrow teaching the old sparrow to fly.*

گوسفند را به گرگ سپردن.

Set not a wolf to keep a sheep.
*Asking a wolf to mind the sheep.*

گوشت را به گربه مسپار.

Never send the dog to deliver a steak.
*Asking a cat to watch the meat.*

گوش شیطون کر.

Keep your fingers crossed.
*Let the devil's ear be shut deaf.*

135

گوشواره عزیز است، گوش عزیزتر است.

Near is my shirt but nearer is my skin.
*The earring is dear, but the ear is dearer.*

گهی پشت به زین و گهی زین به پشت.

You win some you lose some.
*Sometimes your back is on the saddle and sometimes the saddle is on your back.*

136

لایق هر خر نباشد زعفران.

Do not cast pearls before swine.
*Not every ass is worthy of saffron.*

لقمه بزرگتر از دهنت برندار.

Don't bite off more than you can chew.
*Do not take a morsel larger than your mouth.*

لقمه را هم باید جوید و در دهنش گذاشت.

To lie in bed, till meat falls in one's mouth.
*You have to chew his food and put it in his mouth.*

لنگه کفش کهنه در بیابان نعمت خداست.

When nothing is, a little does ease.
*An old shoe in the desert is the blessing of God.*

لیلی را از دریچهٔ چشم مجنون باید دید.

Beauty is in the eye of the beholder.
*You have to see Leyli from the eyes of Majnoon.**

---

* Leyli and Majnoon are classical lovers of Persian and Arabic literature.

م

ما این ورجوی، شما اونور جوی.

Fences make good neighbors.
*We are on this side of the stream, and you are on the other side.*

مأمورم و معذور.

Don't kill the messenger.

مادر با یکدست گهواره را تکان می دهد با دست دیگردنیا را.

The hand that rocks the cradle rules the world.
*The mother rocks the cradle with one hand and the world with the other.*

مار گزیده از ریسمان سیاه و سفید می ترسد.

Once bitten twice shy.
*He that has been bitten by a serpent is afraid of a black and white rope.*

ماستی که ترش است از تغارش پیداست.

Such a beginning, such an end.
*It is apparent from the jug that the yogurt is sour.*

مال از بهر آسایش عمر است، نه عمر از بهر گردآوردن مال.

What we spent we had, what we gave, we have, what we left,
we lost.
*Wealth is for living in comfort, living is not for amassing.*

مال حرام بی برکت است.

Ill gotten good never prospers.

مال خودم مال خودم، مال مردم هم مال خودم.

What's yours is mine and what's mine is my own.
*What is mine is mine, what belongs to others is also mine.*

137

مال دنیا به دنیا می ماند.

You can't take it with you.
*Worldly possession will remain in the world.*

مال را به روی صاحبش خرند.

If you can't smile, don't open a shop.
*A pleasant owner can sell his merchandise.*

ماما که دوتا شد سر بچه کج در میآید.

Too many cooks spoil the broth.
*Where there are two midwives, the baby's head comes out crooked.*

138

ماه همیشه پشت ابر نمی ماند.

Face to face, the truth comes out.
*The moon is not always covered by the clouds.*

ماهی از سرگَنده گردد، نی ز دُم.

Fish begin to stink at the head.
*Fish begins to rot at the head, not at the tail.*

مایهٔ عیش آدمی شکم است.

All grief with bread is less.
*Man's happiness is his belly.*

مبادا که در دهر دیر ایستی

مصیبت بود پیـری و نیستی

A hundred disorders has old age.
*Be mindful of old age and poverty.*

مثل جن و بسم الله.

Oil and water don't mix.
*Like a demon and "In the name of God.* "*

139

مثل خر تو گل مونده.

Stuck between a rock and a hard place.
*He is like a donkey, stuck in the mud.*

مثل سیبی که از وسط دو نصف کرده باشند.

Like two peas in a pod.
*Like an apple cut in half.*

مثل طبل تو خالی می ماند.

Empty vessel makes the most sound.
*He is like an empty drum.*

مثل کَبک سرش را زیر برف کرده.

The cat shut its eyes while it steals cream.
*The partridge puts his head underneath the snow.*

---

* Demons disappear upon the mention of the name of God.

مثل گاو پیشانی سفید می ماند.

As well known as the village water-pump.
*As well known as the cow with the white forehead.*

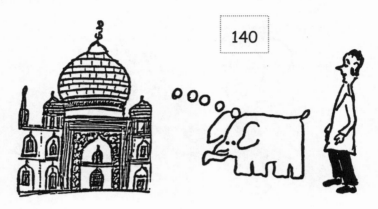

140

مثل گربه مرتضی علی میمونه، از هر جا بیندازی چهار دست و پا میاد پایین.

He's like a cat; fling him whichever way, he'll land on his feet.
*He is like Morteza-Ali's cat; fling him which way you will, he will land on his feet.*

مثل سگ هفت تا جون دارد.

A cat has nine lives.
*Like a dog he has nine lives.*

مردن به عزت به که زندگی به مذلت.

Better to die with honor than to live with shame.

مرده نمیتونه شهادت بده.

Dead men tell no tales.
*The dead cannot be witness.*

مرده آنست که نامش به نکویی نبرند.

Take away my good name and take away my life.
*A dead person is one whose name is remembered in infamy.*

مرغ همسایه غاز است.

The grass is always greener on the other side of the fence.
*The neighbor's chicken appears a goose.*

مرغ یک پا دارد.

Stubborn as a mule.
*The chicken has one leg.*

مرغی را که در هواست نباید به سیخ کشید.

Don't bargain for fish which are still in water.
*The bird in the air cannot be grilled.*

141

مرگ خبر نمی کند.

Death keeps no calendar.
*Death makes no announcements.*

مرگ خر، عروسی سگ است.

One man's breath, another's death.
*The death of the ass makes a feast for the dogs.*

مرگ شتریست که درخونهٔ همه میخوابه.

Death is the black camel that kneels before every door.
*Death is a camel which sleeps in everyone's house.*

142

مرگ فقیر و غنی نمی شناسد.

For who's a prince or beggar in the grave.
*Death does not know poor or rich.*

مرگ میخواهی برو گیلان.

He that has no ill fortune, is troubled with good.
*If you want death go to Gilan.*

مرگ یکبار، شیون هم یکبار.

Better face a danger once than be always in danger.
*Dying once, crying once.*

---

* Gilan was a malaria infected region.

مزد آن گرفت جان برادر که کار کرد.

Diligence is the mother of good fortune.
*He earned wages, dear brother, who worked.*

مزن بی تأمل به گفتـــــار دم

نکو گوی اگر دیر گویی چه غم

Think twice before you speak once.
*Breath not a word without forethought, speak kindly, it matters not if you speak late.*

143

مزهٔ دهن هر کسی فرق می کند.

Everyone to his taste.
*Everyone has a different taste.*

مستمع صاحب سخن را بر سر کار آورد.

The most difficult thing of all, to keep quiet and listen.
*The willing listener encourages the speaker.*

مستی و راستی.

There is truth in wine.
*Drunkenness and truthfulness.*

مسجد نساخته گدا درش ایستاده.

Don't put the cart before the horse.
*The beggar is already standing in front of the unbuilt mosque.*

144

مشت نمونهٔ خروار است.

The sack is known by the sample.
*The fistful is representative of a ton.*

مُشک آنست که خود ببوید، نه آنکه عطار بگوید.

A good wine needs no blush.
*Proof of musk is in the smell, not what the perfume-seller says.*

مشکلی نیست که آسان نشود.

It is a long lane that has no turning.
*There is nothing difficult that cannot be made easy.*

معشوق خوبروی چه محتاج زیور است.

Fair faces need no paint.
*A beautiful sweetheart needs not be adorned.*

مگر از دندهٔ چپ بلند شدی؟

Have you gotten up from the wrong side of the bed?
*Have you gotten up on your left ribs?*

مگر از زیر بته به عمل آمده ام.

I was not raised in a barn.
*I was not raised under the bush.*

مگر پول علف خرس است.

Money does not grow on trees.
*Money is not the bear's grass.*

مگر در خواب ببینی.

Wishful thinking.
*You may only see it in your dream.*

145

مگر کف دستم را بو کرده ام.

How on the earth would I know?
*Have I have smelled my palm?*

مگر هالو گیر آورده ای؟

I was not born yesterday.

146

من از بیـــگانگان هرگــز ننالـــم
که با من هرچه کرد آن آشنا کرد

Save us from our friends!
*I never complain about strangers,*
*whatever bad happened was at the hand of friends.*

منتظران را بلب آمد نفس.

To one who waits, a moment seems a year.
*For those who wait, their breath comes to their mouth.*

منع چو بیند حریص تر شود انسان.

Forbidden fruit is sweet.
*Man wants what is forbidden.*

من که به هر ساز تو می رقصم.

You play the tune, I'll do the dance.
*I dance to every tune you play.*

**من که شدم از دنیا بدر، دنیا شود زیر و زبر.**

When I am gone let happen what may.
*When I have left the world, let it turn upside down.*

**من نه سر پیازم نه ته پیاز.**

It is none of my business.
*I am neither the top nor the bottom of the onion.*

**من، یک من، تو هم یک من، پس کی نیم من؟**

I proud, and you proud, who shall bear the ashes out?

**مورچگان را چو بـــود اتفـــاق**

**شیر ژیـــان را بدرانند پوست**

United we stand, divided we fall.
*When ants unite, they can skin a lion.*

147

**موش تو سوراخ نمیرفت، جارو به دمش می بست.**

You needed this like you needed a hole in the head.
*The mouse couldn't get into the hole, yet he tied a broom to his tail.*

می خواهی بخواه، نمی خواهی نخواه.

Take it or leave it.

میهمان تا سه روز عزیز است.

Fish and house guests smell in three days.
*Guests are appreciated for three days.*

میهمان سخت عزیز است ولی همچو نفس
خفه میسازد اگر آید و بیـــرون نـــــرود

First day a guest, the second day a guest, the third day a
calamity.
*Guest are dear, but they can be suffocating like a breath if they
come and not leave.*

میهمان ناخوانده خرجش با خودش است.

He who comes uncalled, sits unserved.
*An uninvited guest should pay for his expenses.*

148

میازار موری کـه دانـــــه کــش است
که جان دارد و جان شیرین خـوش است

If you want to live and thrive, let the spider run alive.
*Don't hurt the ant carrying it's seeds, its life is as sweet.*

میان ماه من تا ماه گـــــــردون

تفاوت از زمین تا آسمان است

There is some difference between Peter and Peter.
*There is a difference between my moon and the one in the sky.*

149

میخاد از جوی بگذره، پاش هم خیس نشه.

The cat would eat fish and would not wet her feet.
*He wants to cross the stream without his feet getting wet.*

می خواهی عزیز باشی یا دور شو یا گور شو.

Familiarity breeds contempt.
*If you wish to become dear, either die or stay away.*

میمونک هرچی زشت تره، بازیش بیشتره.

The worst wheel of a cart makes the worst noise.
*The uglier the monkey, the more its mimicry.*

میون دعوا حلوا خیر نمی کنند.

Revolutions are not made with rose water.
*They don't offer halvah at fights.*

نابرده رنج گنج میسر نمی شود.

No pain, no gain.
*Wealth cannot be obtained without toil.*

نادان را بهتر از خاموشی نیست.

If the fool knew how to be silent he could sit among the wise.
*For an ignorant person there is nothing better than silence.*

نام نیک رفتگان ضایع مکن.

Speak only what's true of the living and what is honorable of the dead.
*Do not destroy the good name of the dead.*

نام نیکو گر بماند ز آدمی
به کزو ماند سرای زرنگار

A good name is better than riches.
*It is better to leave a good name than a castle of gold.*

نان برکت خداست.

Bread is the staff of life.
*Bread is God's blessing.*

نان را به نرخ روز می خورد.

Other times, other manners.
*He eats bread at the ruling market price.*

نانش توی روغن است.

His bread is buttered on both sides.
*His bread has been dipped in oil.*

نبرد رگی تا خدا نخواهد.

What God will, no frost can kill.

150

نخود هر آش است.

He has his finger in every pie.
*He is the pea of every soup.*

ندهد نقد را به نسیه کسی.

Better a sparrow in the hand than a pigeon on the roof.
*No one will give up the ready for that which is yet to come.*

نردبام پله پله.

He who would climb the ladder, must begin at the bottom.
*Climb the ladder one step at a time.*

نشود بز به پِچ و پِچ فربه.

Praise without profit puts little in the pot.
*The goat does not get fat just by whispering.*

نفاق بینداز و حکومت کن.

Divide and rule.

نکبت نیامده را نباید استقبال کرد.

Don't fear the worst until you see the worst.
*One should not welcome misfortune.*

151

نگاه به دست ننه کن، مثل ننه غربیله کن.

Like mother, like daughter.
*Watch the mother's hand and sift like her.*

نگو تا نشنوی.

One ill word asks another.

نم پس نمیده.

You can't get blood out of stone.

152

نمک خوری نمکدان نشکن.

Don't bite the hand that feeds you.
*To eat salt and break the salt shaker.*

نوبتی هم باشد نوبت ماست.

Turnabout is fair play.
*If it's someone's turn, it's my turn.*

نوشدارو بعد از مرگ سهراب.

While men go after a leech, the body is buried.
*Medicine comes after the death of Sohrab.*

نوکرمون نوکری داشت، نوکرشم چوکری داشت.

You're a lady, I'm a lady, who will milk the cow?
*My servant had a servant, who himself had a servant.*

---

\* Sohrab was the son of Rostam in Iranian mythology. In the most well known story he receives aid only after he is dead.

نوش با نیش است.

No joy without alloy.

153

نوکر نو تیز رو.

A new broom sweeps clean.
*A new servant walks fast.*

نـو که اومد به بـازار
کهنه میـشه دل آزار

Out with the old, in with the new.
*When new wares appear in the market, the old becomes*
*annoying.*

نومید دلیر باشد.

Despair gives courage to a coward.

نون بده فرمون بده.

All things are obedient to money.
*Pay first then give orders.*

نونت را با آب بخور، منت آبدوغ نکش.

Better go to bed without supper than to rise in debt.

*Eat your bread with water and don't ask for another's doogh.**

نه به این شوری شور، نه به اون بی نمکی.

Too much spoils, too little does not satisfy.

*Not so highly salted as that, nor so insipid as that.*

نه چندان بخور کــز دهانت بر آید

نه چندان که از ضعف جانت بر آید

Eat to live, not live to eat.

*Eat neither so much that the food may come out of your mouth,
nor so little that weakness may cause your life to depart.*

154

نه خود خورم نه کس دهم گَنده کنم به سگ دهم.

Like the gardener's dog, that neither eats cabbages himself nor
lets anybody else.

*I will not eat it myself, nor give it to another, I let it go bad and
give it to the dogs.*

---

* A drink made from yogurt.

نه راه پس هست نه راه پیش.

Stuck between a rock and a hard place.
*There is no way to go forward or backward.*

155

نه قم خوبه نه کاشون لعنت به هر دو تاشون.

No choice among stinking fish.
*Qum is no good. Neither is Kashan. Damn them both.**

نه هر که به صورت نکوست، سیرت زیبا در اوست.

The handsomest flower is not the sweetest.
*Not all that has a beautiful face has a good spirit.*

نه همین لباس زیباست نشان آدمیت.

It is not the gay coat that makes the gentleman.
*Nice clothes are not the sign of humanity.*

نیارد شاخ بد جز تخم بد بار.

Figs do not grow thistles.
*From a bad seed comes a bad sapling.*

---

* Qum and Kashan are towns in Iran.

نیست بالاتر از سیاهی رنگ.

There is no color above black.


نیش عقرب نه از ره کین است

اقتضای طبیعتــــــش اینست

What can you expect from a pig but a grunt.
*The scorpions sting not from spite but of nature.*


نیش قلم تیزتر از تیغ دو دم.

The pen is mightier than the sword.
*The nib of pen is sharper than a razor.*


نیم حکیم بلای جان، نیم فقیه بلای ایمان.

A little knowledge is a dangerous thing.
*A half-learned physician is a danger to life, and a half-learned mullah is a danger to faith.*

156

و

واکن کیسه، بخور هریسه.

Pay the piper and call the tune.
*Loosen your purse and eat porridge.*

وجود ناقص به از عدم محض است.

Better an eye sore than all blind.
*A crippled body is better than none.*

وصله ناهمرنگ به از سوراخ باز است.

Half a loaf is better than none.
*An ill-matched patch is better than an uncovered hole.*

وطـن آنجـاست کازاری نباشد

کسی را با کسـی کـاری نباشد

Where it is well with me, there is my country.
*Home is where there is no harm,*
*where no one bothers no one.*

وعدهٔ سر خرمن دادن.

If the sky falls, we shall catch larks.

وقت احتیاج باید دم خر را هم بوسید.

It is better to kiss a knave than to be troubled with him.
*In necessity, one may kiss the ass's tail.*

وقت طلاست.

Time is money.
*Time is gold.*

وقتیکه جیک جیک مستونت بود یاد زمستونت نبود؟

In fair weather, prepare for fall.
*Oh, little bird, when you were singing happily, you did not
think of winter.*

157

هر آشپزی یک جور آش می پزد.

Everyone to his taste.
*Every cook has his own way of making soup.*

هر آن سری که داری با دوست در میان مَنه، چه دانی که وقتی که دشمن گردد.

Tell nothing to thy friend that thine enemy not know.
*Tell not your friends your secrets. They may become your foes.*

هر آنکس که دندان دهد نان دهد.

God never sends mouth without sending meat.
*Whoever gives teeth, also sends bread.*

هر آنکه را عقل هست و مالش نیست
روزی آن عـقـل بالشـــــــی دهدش

Better wit than wealth.
*He who has wisdom and no money, someday that wisdom will comfort him.*

هر ابری بارون نداره.

All clouds bring not rain.

هر بهاری را خزانی در پی است.

No summer but has its winter.
*Every summer leads to fall.*

158

هر جا دود هست آتش هم هست.

Where there is smoke, there is fire.

هر چه آسان بدست آید، آسان هم از دست می رود.

Easy come easy go.
*What is gained easily, is lost easily.*

هر چه از دوست میرسد نیکوست.

It is the thought that counts.
*Whatever comes from a friend is good.*

هر چه بادا باد.

What will be will be.

هرچه بار کمتر، راحت تر.

Little wealth, little care.
*The lighter the load, the more the comfort.*

159

هر چه بسیار شود خوار شود.

One ceases to appreciate a thing when one has a surfeit of it.
*Anything in great supply is despised.*

هرچه به همش بزنی گندش بیشتر در می آید.

The more you stir turd, the more it stinks.
*The more you stir, the more it stinks.*

هرچه پول بدی همانقدر آش می خوری.

Pay the piper and call the tune.
*You eat as much soup as you pay for.*

هرچه پیش آید خوش آید.

All is for the best.

هر چه در دیگ است به چمچه در میآید.

Nothing comes out of the sack but what was in it.
*What is in the pot will come out in the ladle.*

هر چه دیر آید خوش آید.

Late is often lucky.
*Whatever comes late, comes lucky.*

هر چه رِشتیم پنبه شد.

My cake is dough.
*Whatever I had spun is turned into cotton.*

هر چه زود آید نپاید.

Soon gotten, soon spent.
*Whatever comes quickly, does not last.*

160

هر چه سر بزرگتر، درد سر بزرگتر.

Greater tree attracts wind.
*The bigger the head, the bigger the headache.*

هر چه عوض دارد گله ندارد.

A fair exchange is no robbery.

161

هرچه کمیاب است با ارزش تراست.

That thing which is rare is dear.

هرچه کنی به خود کنی

نیـک و یا که بــد کنی

Like fault, like punishment.
*Whether good or bad, you do it to yourself.*

هر چیز چاره داره جز مرگ.

There is a remedy for everything but death.

هر چیزی به موقعش خوبست.

Everything is good in its season.
*Everything at the proper time is good.*

هرچیز که خوار آید یکروز به کار آید.

What is despised today will be useful tomorrow.

هر که را طاووس خواهد جور هندوستان کشد.

He that would have the fruit must climb the tree.
*He who wants a peacock must suffer India.*

هر حاجی یک جور مکه می رود.

There is more than one way to skin a cat.
*Each Hajji\* goes to Mecca his own way.*

هر حرف راستی را نباید گفت.

All truths are not to be told.

هر خوردنی پس دادنی دارد.

One good turn deserves another.
*Every entertainment needs to be reciprocated.*

162

هر روز عید نیست که حلوا خورد کسی.

Christmas comes but once a year.
*Not every day is a holiday when we can eat halvah.*

---

\* Someone who has done pilgrimage to Mecca.

هر روز گاو نمی میرد تا کوفته ارزان شود.

We don't kill a pig every day.
*It Is not everyday a cow dies so meatball goes cheap.*

163

هر سخن جایی و هر نکته مکانی دارد.

There is a time and place for everything.
*Every word has its place and every remark has its occasion.*

هر سگی تو لونهٔ خودش شیر است.

Every dog is a lion at home.

هر ضرری عقلی را زیاده کند.

Adversity makes a man wise, not rich.
*Every loss makes you wiser.*

هر ضرری منفعتی دارد.

No great loss but some small profit.
*Every loss has some profit.*

هرطرف که باد آید بادش دهد.

Pull down your hat on the wind side.
*He turns his mill with the wind's direction.*

هر عروسی تا چهل روز سفید بخت است.

Everything new is fine.
*Every bride is happy for forty days.*

هر عیب که سلطان بپسندد هنر است.

Fair is not fair, but that which pleases.
*Every vice that the king approves is a virtue.*

هر فرازی را نشیبی است.

What goes up, must come down.
*Every rise has a dip.*

164

هر که ظالمی را از بند رهاند، خود در بند بماند.

Cruelty deserves no mercy.
*He who frees and oppressor from jail, will remain oppressed.*

هر کجا درد است درمانش مقرر کرده اند.

The hand that gave the wound must give the cure.
*For every pain there is a cure.*

هر کجا روی آسمان همین رنگ است.

Nothing is new under the sun.
*Wherever you go, the sky is the same color.*

هر کسی چند روزه نوبت اوست.

Every dog has his day.
*Everyone has his turn for a few days.*

هر کس را فرزند خویش خوش نماید.

There is only one pretty child in the world, and every mother
has it.
*Every child looks beautiful to his parents.*

165

هر کسی سخن نسنجد از جواب برنجد.

He that speaks the thing he should not, hears the thing he
would not.

هر کسی دردش در دل خودش است.

No one knows the weight of another's man's burden.
*Everyone's pain is in his heart.*

هر کسی را بهر کاری ساختند.

Every man must labor in his own trade.
*Everyone is made to do something.*

هر کس کسیرا می خواهد سگش را هم می خواهد.

Love me, love my dog.
*If you love someone, you should love his dog.*

هر کسی از صدای خودش خوشش می آید.

Every ass loves to hear himself bray.
*Everyone is fond of his own voice.*

هر که از چشم دور، از دل دور.

Long absent, soon forgotten.
*Out of sight, out of heart.*

هر که آمد عمارتی نو ساخت

رفت و منزل بدیگری پرداخت

Today a man, tomorrow none.
*Everyone who comes into the world erects a new building,*
*he departs and leaves it to another.*

167

هر که آن کند که نباید، آن بیند که نشاید.

He that does what he should not shall feel what he would not.

هرکه افزون خواهد باید از درد و رنج نترسد.

No bees no honey, no work, no money.
*He who wants more should not be afraid of pain and suffering.*

هر که او بیدارتر، پر درد تر.

Much science, much sorrow.
*He who is more awake, is in more pain.*

هر که اول بنگـرد پایان کـار

اندر آخر او نگردد شرمسار

Forethought is easy, repentance hard.
*He who thinks of the end at the beginning,*
*will not be sorry at the end.*

هر که با بزرگان ستیزد، خون خود بریزد.

The fly that plays too long in the candle, singes his wings at last.
*He who fights with the powerful, sheds his own blood.*

هر که با رسوا نشیند عاقبت رسوا شود.

If you lie down with dogs, you will get up with fleas.

هر که بامش بیش برفش بیشتر.

God gives the shoulder according to the burden.
*The bigger the roof the more snow it gets.*

168

هر که به امید همسایه نشست، شب گرسنه می خوابد.

He who depends on another, dines ill and sups worse.
*He who depends on his neighbor, sleeps hungry at night.*

هر که ترسید مرد، هر که نترسید برد.

Nothing ventured, nothing gained.
*He that was in fear, died. He who did not, won.*

هر که تنها به قاضی رود راضی برمی گردد.

The absent are always in the wrong.
*Who that goes to the judge alone returns happy.*

هر که چیزی ندارد غمی ندارد.

Small riches hath most rest.
*He who has nothing, has no worries.*

هر که خر به بام برد فرود تواند آورد.

He that has his hand in the lion's mouth, must take it out as
well as he can.
*He who took the ass to the roof, can take him down.*

169

هر که خوابست قسمتش به آب است.

He who sleeps all morning, may go a begging all the day after.
*The portion of him who goes to sleep goes on the water.*

هر که دست از جان شوید

هر چـه در دل دارد بگوید

When death is on the tongue, repentance is not difficult.
*He who has no hope of life, will say whatever is in his heart.*

170

هر که درقمار شانس دارد در عشق شانس ندارد.

Lucky at cards, unlucky at love.
*He who is lucky in gambling, is unlucky in love.*

هر که را زر در ترازوست، زور در بازوست.

He that has money has what he wants.
*He who has gold on the scale, has strength in his arms.*

هر که را در عقل او نقصان فتاد

کار او فی الجـــمله آسان اوفتاد

Children and fools have merry lives.
*He who is not smart has an easy life.*

هر که را در سر نباشد عشق یار

بهر او پالان و افســــاری بیار

He that does not love a woman, sucked a sow.
*Whoever has never been in love, bring him a saddle and bridle.*

171

هر که راز خود به گوشــی باز گفت

ترجمان از صد زبان خواهد شنفت

Confide in an aunt and the world will know.
*He who tells his secret to one ear,*
*will hear it from a thousand tongues.*

هر که عیب دگران نزد تو آورد و شمـــرد

به یقین عیب تو پیش دگران خواهد برد

Who chatters to you will chatter of you.
*He who told you of other's faults,*
*will surely tell others of your faults.*

هر که قانع تر آسوده تر.

The greatest wealth is contentment with a little.
*The more content, the more relaxed.*

هر که را مال هست و عقلش نیست
روزی آن مال مالشی دهدش

Without wisdom, wealth is worthless.
*He who has money but no wisdom, one day the money will bring him pain.*

هر که را میخواهی بشناسی یا با او معامله کن یا سفر.

A man knows his companion in a long way and a little inn.
*If you want to know a person do business or travel with him.*

172

هر که را خلقش نکو نیکش شمار
خواه از نسل علی خواه از عمر

Handsome is that handsome does.
*Consider him good who's nature is good, be he a follower of Ali or of Omar.*

هر که رو داری کرد، خانه داری نکند.

The more women look in their glass, the less they look to their
house.
*She who take's care of her face, takes not care of her house.*

173

هر که ریش داشت با نیست.

All that glitters is not gold.
*Not everything with a beard is your dad.*

هر که زن ندارد، آرام تن ندارد.

A man without a wife is but half a man.
*He who has no wife is not settled.*

هر که طاووس خواهد جور هندوستان کشد.

He that would have fruit must climb the tree.
*He who wants a peacock must suffer to India.*

هر که مال ندارد یار ندارد.

When poverty comes in at the door, love flies out of the window.
*He who has no money has no sweet heart.*

هرکی با آتش بازی کند باید انتظار سوختن هم داشته باشد.

If you play with fire, you will get burnt.

هرکی به فکر خویشه، کوسه به فکر ریشه.

Every man draws the water to his own mill.
*Everyone thinks for himself, and the thin-bearded man thinks of improving his beard.*

هرکی تهی کیسه تر، آسوده تر.

Small riches hath most rest.
*The more empty the sack the more rest.*

هرکی خربزه می خورد پای لرزش هم می نشیند.

If you play with fire you'll get burnt.
*He who eats Persian melon, must take the risk of shivering too.*

174

هرکی خیال میکند بچهٔ خودش از همه خوشگلتر است.

The owl thinks her own young fairest.
*Everyone thinks his own child is the fairest.*

هرکی دستش سرد است، قلبش گرم است.

Cold hands, warm heart.

175

هر گردویی گرد است ولی هر گِردی گردو نیست.

All that glitters is not gold.
*Everything that is round is not a walnut.*

هر گلی بوی خودش را دارد.

Each flower has its own smell.

هر مالی نرخی دارد.

Everything has a price.

هِر و از بِر تمیز نمیده.

He knows not a pig from a dog.
*He doesn't know an "h" from a "b."*

هزار دوست کم است و یک دشمن بسیار.

One enemy is too many, a hundred friends too few.

هزار وعده خوبان یکی وفا نکند.

He that promises too much means nothing.
*A thousand promises of the beauty counts not for one truth.*

هشتتش گرو نُه اش است.

He that has but four and spends five, has no need of a purse.
*His "eight" is in hock for his "nine."*

هم آش معاویه را میخوره، هم نماز علی را میخونه.

You can't run with the hare and hunt with the hounds.
*He eats with Moavieh and prays with Ali.**

هم از توبره میخوره، هم از آخور.

He wants to have it both ways.

176

هم حلوای مرده هاست هم خورش زنده ها.

You can't run with the hare and hunt with the hounds.
*He is the "halvah" of the dead, and the "stew" of the living.*

---

\* Moavieh, a caliph was an enemy of Ali, the leader of the Shi'is.

هم خدا را میخاد و هم خرما را.

You can't have your cake and eat it too.
*He wants both God and dates.*

177

هم خرما هم ثواب.

Both a duty and a pleasure.
*Both dates and spiritual rewards.*

همسایه نیک در جهان فضل خداست.

A good neighbor, a good morrow.
*A good neighbor in this world is a blessing.*

همکار، همکار را نمی تواند ببیند.

One potter envies another.
*One colleague cannot bear the other.*

همه کاره و هیچکاره.

Jack of all trades and master of none.
*Does everything and does nothing.*

همنشینم به شود، تا من از او بهتر شوم.

The good man makes others good.
*My company should be good, so that I may be better than him.*

178

همه قماش آدمی تو دنیا پیدا می شود.

It takes all sorts to make a world.
*There are all kinds of people in the world.*

همیشه حق با مشتری است.

The customer is always right.

همیشه شعبون، یکدفعه رمضون.

Always the brides maid, never the bride.
*Should it always be Sha'ban? Let it once be Ramazan.*

همین هلو است و همین گلو.

The same old story in the same old way.
*It is the same peach and the same throat.*

---

* Two months in the Muslim calendar.

هِندوانه زیر بغل کسی گذاشتن.

To lay it on thick.
*To put watermelon under someone's arm.*

179

هنر چشمهٔ زاینده است و دولت پاینده.

An artist lives everything.
*Art is a living fountain and an everlasting fortune.*

هنوز مسجد ساخته نشده کور بر درش نشسته.

Don't build the sty before the litter comes.
*The mosque is yet built, yet the blind man is sitting at its door.*

هیچ جا مثل خونهٔ آدم نمیشه.

There is no place like home.

هیچ دویی نیست که سه نشه.

Third time lucky.
*There is no "two" which does not become a "three."*

هیچ کس از شکم مادر عالم زائیده نشده.

None is born a master.
*No one came out of his mother's womb a wise man.*

هیچ گرانی بی علت نیست و هیچ ارزانی بی حکمت.

Good and cheap is dear.
*There is nothing costly without a reason,*
*and nothing cheap without a wisdom.*

هیچکس محل سگ هم به او نمی گذارد.

It is a poor dog that is not worth whistling for.
*He gets less attention than a dog gets.*

یا دوستی صادق، یا دشمنی ظاهر.

Better an open enemy than a false friend.
*A sincere friend or an open enemy.*

یا رب مباد آنکه گدا معتبر شود.

Set a beggar on horseback; he will ride to the devil.
*O' God! don't let a beggar become wealthy.*

یا سر میرود یا کلاه میاید.

Either you lose the saddle or win the horse.
*Either you lose your head or win the hat.*

یاری که تحمل نکند یار نباشد.

A good friend never offends.
*A friend who is not tolerant is not a friend.*

یاسین بگوش خر خواندن.

To play a lyre to an ass.
*To read the chapter of Yaseen* in an ass's ear.*

---

* A verse from the Koran.

یا مکن با پیلبانان دوستـــــی
یا بنا کن خانه ای در خورد پیل

He that sups with the devil must have a long spoon.
*Either you should not make friends with the elephant driver, or*
*you should build a house fit for the elephant.*

یک آب خوش از گلویم پائین نرفته.

No day passes without some grief.
*A pleasant bit of water has not gone down my throat.*

یک ارباب و ده نوکر شنیده بودیم اما یک نوکر و ده ارباب نشنیده بودیم.

No man can serve two masters.
*We had heard about one master and ten servants, but not*
*about one servant and ten masters.*

181

یک ارزن از دستش نمی افتد.

He won't give away the droppings of his nose.
*A seed won't fall from his hand.*

یک بار جستی ملخک؛

دو بـــار جستی ملخک؛

آخر به دستی ملخک.

Punishment is lame, but it comes.
*You jumped away once, little locust;*
*you jumped away twice, little locust;*
*finally someone caught you, little locust.*

یک بزگر گله را گر میکند.

One scabbed sheep will mar a whole flock.
*A scabbed sheep is enough for the whole flock.*

یک پایش لب گور است.

To have one foot in the grave.
*His foot is at the edge of the grave.*

یک پول جگرک سفره قلمکار نمیخاد.

The game is not worth the candle.

یک جو رو از ده شِشدانگی بهتر است.

Fortune favors bold.
*A grain of boldness is worth more than a village.*

یک حمام خرابه چهل جامه دار نمیخاد.

Eleven grooms for a one eyed horse!
*A rundown bathhouse does not need forty attendants.*

یک دست صدا نداره.

Two heads are better than one.
*One hand makes no noise.*

یک روز من بیمار می شدم، یه روز معلم، یه روز من حموم می رفتم، یه روز

معلم، یه روز من لباس می شستم، یه روز معلم، روز هفتم هم جمعه بود!*

Everyday is a holiday with sluggards.

یک سال بخور نون و تره، صد سال بخور نون وکره.

He that saves his dinner will have the more for his supper.
*Eat bread and leeks for a year, then eat bread and butter for a hundred years.*

182

یک سوزن به خودت بزن و یک جوالدوز به مردم.

What is good for the goose is good for the gander.
*Prick yourself with a sewing needle before pricking others with a packing needle.*

یک سیب را که به آسمان بیندازی، چندین چرخ می خوره تا بزمین برگردد.

There is many a slip between the cup and the lip.
*An apple thrown into the air turns a thousand times before it falls back to the ground.*

---

\* جواب پسری به پدرش که او را برای تحصیل به
شهر فرستاده بود و عاقبت بیسواد برگشت.

یک گنجشک در دست بهتر از ده گنجشک در هوا است.

A bird in the hand is worth two in the bush.
*A sparrow in hand is better than ten in the air.*

یکی بچه گـرگ مـی پــرورید

چـو پرورده شد خواجه را بردرید

He brought up a bird to pick out his own eyes.
*He raised a wolf cub, when it grew up it devoured him.*

یکی چهارشنبه پول گم میکنه، یکی پول پیدا میکنه.

One man's loss is another man's gain.
*One Wednesday one loses money, one find money.*

مثل ۱۰۰۱

یک هزار و یک مثل آ ورده ام

هر مثل گویا تر از صد داستـان

May "1001 Proverbs" bring you delight,
more than the stories of the "1001 Nights."

# ENGLISH BIBLIOGRAPHY

Abrishami, Ahmad. *A Dictionary of Persian-English Proverbs.* Tehran: Zivar Publications, 1997.

Akbar, Fatollah. *The Eye of an Ant.* Bethesda, Maryland: IBEX Publishers, 1995.

Collis, Harry. *American Proverbs.* Lincolnwood: Passport Books, 1992.

Fergusson, Rosalind. *The Penguin Dictionary of Proverbs.* New York: Market House Books Ltd., 1983.

Haim, Soleyman. *Persian-English Proverbs.* Tehran: Brookhim Booksellers, 1334.

Meider, Wolfgang. *The Prentice Hall Encyclopedia of Proverbs.* Englewood Cliffs, New Jersey: Prentice Hall, Inc., 1986.

Simpson, John. *The Concise Oxford Dictionary of Proverbs.* New York: Oxford University Press, 1983.

————. *The Oxford Dictionary of English Proverbs.* Oxford: Clarendon Press, 1970.

*The Holy Bible.* Michigan: Zondervan Bible Publishers, 1984.

Titelman, Gregory Y. *Random House Dictionary of Proverbs and Sayings.* New York: Random House, 1956.

# فهرست منابع مثل های فارسی

آذرلی، غلامرضا. **ضرب المثل های مشهور ایران**. تهران: انتشارات ارغوان.

اردشیرجی، شاپور. **فرهنگ اصطلاحات روزمره انگلیسی و آمریکائی.**

امینی، امیرقلی. **فرهنگ عوام یا تغییر اصطلاحات پارسی.** تهـران: مؤسسـهٔ مطبوعـاتی علی اکبر علمی.

جمشیدی پور، یوسف. **ضرب المثل های شیرین فارسی**. تهران، انتشارات فروغی، ۱۳۶۹.

خدایار، امیر مسعود. **اندرزها و مثل های مصطلح در زبان فارسی**. تهران.

سهیلی، مهدی. **ضرب المثل های معروف ایران**. تهران: انتشارات شرق، ۱۳۷۱.

عظیمـی، صـادق. **فرهنـگ مثلها و اصطلاحـات متـداول در زبـان فارسـی**. لنـدن: چـاپ و نشر پیام، ۱۳۶۹.

دهخدا، علی اکبر. **لغتنامهٔ دهخدا**. تهران، دانشگاه تهران، ۱۳۳۷.

وکیلیان، احمد. **تمثیل و مثل** (جلد دوّم). تهران: انتشارات سروش، ۱۳۶۶.

# KEY TO ILLUSTRATED PROVERBS
## جواب مثل ها و اصطلاحات مصوّر

1- Even an ass does not fall in a pit twice.

حتی خر هم دو بار پایش در یک چاله نمی رود.

2- He who digs a pit for another, falls in himself.

چاه مکن بهر کسی/ اول خودت دوم کسی.

3- Necessity is the mother of invention.

احتیاج مادر اختراع است.

4- Don't bite off more than you can chew.

لقمه بزرگتر از دهانت برندار.

5- Divide and rule.

تفرقه بینداز و حکومت کن.

6- The hand that rocks the cradle, rules the world.

مادر با یکدست دنیا را تکان میدهد و با یکدست دنیا را.

7- Diamonds are girl's best friend.

پیوند زن با طلا نا گسستنی است.

8- Don't kill the messenger.

مأمور و معذور.

9- The grass is always greener on the other side of the fence.

چمن همسایه سبزتر است.

10- A swallow does not a summer make.

با یک پرستو تابستان نمیاید.

11- Friends may meet, but mountains never.

کوه به کوه نمیرسد، آدم به آدم می رسد.

12- The pot calling the kettle black.

دیگ به دیگ میگه روت سیاه.

13- A bird in the hand is better than two in the bush.

یک گنجشک در دست بهتر ازده گنجشک در هواست.

14-To play a lyre to an ass.

یاسین بگوش خر خواندن.

15-Late children, early orphans.

بچه سر پیری زنگولهٔ پای تابوت است.

16-Laugh and the world laughs with you.

بخند تا دنیا با تو بخندد.

17-Don't count your chickens before they hatch.

جوجه را آخر پائیز می شمرند.

18-Give a fool enough rope and he'll hang himself.

طناب مجانی هم ببیند خودشرا دار می زند.

19-He that will steal an egg, will steal an ox.

تخم مرغ دزد شتر دزد میشود.

20-Don't cut the branch you're standing on.

تیشه به ریشه خود زدن.

21-Stretch your legs according to your coverlet.

پاتو به اندازهٔ گلیمت دراز کن.

22-The more women look in their glass, the less they look to their houses.

یا آینه داری یا خانه داری

23-No pain, no gain.

نا برده رنج گنج میسر نمیشود

مزد آن گرفت جان برادر که کار کرد.

24-The dog barks in vain at the moon.

مه فشاند نور و سگ عو عو کند.

25-Water spilled on the ground cannot be gathered up again.

آب ریخته جمع شدنی نیست.

26-Bitter pills may have blessed effects.

شفا بایدت داروی تلخ نوش.

27-It is good fishing in troubled water.

از آب گل آلود ماهی گرفتن.

28-The sun shines upon all alike.

آفتاب بر بام همه یکسان می تابد.

29-One man's loss is another man's gain.

یکی چهارشنبه پول پیدا میکنه، یکی پول گم میکنه.

30-One thief robs another.

دزد به دزد میزنه.

31-Physician, heal thyself.

کل اگر طبیب بودی سر خود دوا نمودی.

32-Cats eat what hussies spare.

روزی گربه دست زن شلخته است.

33-He refuses with the right hand and takes with the left. با دست پس میزنه با پا پیش میکشه.

34-All roads lead to Rome. همه راهها به رم ختم میشود.

35-Sadness and gladness succeed each other. در پس هر گریه آخر خنده ایست.

36-No summer but has its winter. هر بهاری را خزانی در پی است.

37-For mad words, deaf ears. جواب ابلهان خاموشی است.

38-Every medal has it's reverse. هر سکه دو روی دارد.

39-No rose without a thorn. گل بی خار نمیشه.

40-One flower makes no garden. با یک گل بهار نمیشه.

41-Rejoice not in other's sorrow. تو کز محنت دیگران بی غمی نشاید که نامت نهند آدمی

42-In the country of blind, the one eyed man is king. در شهر کوران، یک چشمی پادشاه است.

43-The great fish eats up the small fish. ماهی بزرگ ماهی کوچک را می خورد.

44-Blind man will not thank you for a looking glass. آینه داری در مجلس کوران.

45-Dogs bark, the caravan passes. سگ لاید و کاروان گذرد.

46-Sit in your place and no one can make you rise. جایی بنشین که بر نخیزانندت.

47-If God closes a door, he opens a window. خدا گر ز حکمت ببندد د دری ز رحمت گشاید در دیگری.

48-It is not the gay coat that makes the gentleman. نه همین لباس زیباست نشان آدمیت.

49-Even if we study to old age, we shall not finishing learning. ز گهواره تا گور دانش بجوی.

50-Beggers can't be choosers. آدم گدا اینهمه ادا.

51-Absence makes the heart grow fonder. دوری و دوستی.

52-One scabbed sheep will mar a whole flock. یک بز گر گله را گر میکند.

53-Don't steal the minaret before you have dug a pit to hide it in.

اول چاه را بکن بعد منار را بدزد.

54-Every ass loves to hear himself sing.

هر کسی از صدای خودش خوشش میاد.

55-He that is once born, once must die.

آدم یکبار به دنیا میاد و یکبار هم از دنیا

میره.

56-A pot that belongs to many is ill stirred and worse boiled.

دیگ شراکت به جوش نیاید.

57-One barber shaves another gratis.

سلمانی ها وقتی بیکار میشوند، سر

همدیگر را میتراشند.

58-Burying one's head in the sand. (The partridge puts his head underneath the snow.)

مثل کبک سرش را توی برف کرده.

59-Death is the black camel that kneels before every door.

مرگ شتری است که در منزل همه می

خوابد.

60-Think before you speak.

اول اندیشه وانگهی گفتار.

61-It is the raised stick that makes the dog obey.

تا نباشد چوب تر، فرمان نبرد گاو و خر.

62-One flower does not make a garden.

با یک گل بهار نمیشه.

63-Never speak ill of the dead.

پشت سر مرده نباید حرف زد.

64-What goes up must come down.

فواره چون بلند شود سرنگون شود.

65-To walk with a walking stick.

دست به عصا راه رفتن.

66-Every ascent, has a descent.

هر سر بالایی یک سر پائینی داره.

67-Fences make good neighbors.

ما اینور جوی، شما آنور جوی.

68-Cut off a dog's tail and he will be a dog still.

سگ به دریای هفتگانه بشوی، چونکه تر

شد پلید تر باشد.

69-Don't wash your dirty linen in public.

دعوای توی خانه را نباید سر کوچه برد.

70-Scratch my back and I'll scratch yours.

به یکدیگر نان قرض دادن.

71-Stuck between a rock and a hard place. مثل خر تو گل مونده.

72-Don't cry over spilled milk.

بر گذشته حسرت خوردن خطاست.

73-When pigs fly. وقت گل نی.

74-Money does not grow on tree. پول علف خرس نیست.

75-Out of the frying pan and into the fire.

از چاله درآمد و به چاه افتاد.

76-He is rolling in money.

پولش از پارو بالا میره.

77-You can't teach an old dog new tricks.

اسبی را که در چهل سالگی سوغان گیرند،

میدان قیامت را شاید.

78-To wear your heart on your sleeve. سفره دلش پیش همه باز است.

79-He that would have fruit must climb the tree.

هر که طاووس خواهد جور هندوستان

کشد.

80-To put the cart before the horse. سرنا را از سر گشادش زدن.

81-It is the thought that counts.

دوست مرا یاد کند ولو به یک هل پوچ.

82-An ass is most pleasing to another ass.

دیوانه چو دیوانه ببیند خوشش آید.

83-A cracked bell never sounds well.

شیشه بشکسته را پیوند کردن مشکل

است.

84-A watched pot will never boil.

85-Pouring oil on the fire is not the way to quench it.

آتش را به روغن نتواند نشاند.

86-When the fox cannot reach the grapes, he says they are not ripe.

گربه دستش به گوشت نمی رسه، میگه

پیف پیف چه بو میده.

87-It is the last drop that makes the cup run over.

88-Honey catches more flies than vinegar.

با زبان خوش مار را میشود از سوراخ

بیرون کشید.

89-Birds of a feather, flock together.

کبوتر با کبوتر باز با باز

کند همجنس با همجنس پرواز.

90-Watch out, the wind may take your hat.

بپا کلاهت را باد نبره.

91-When there is no water, he is a good swimmer.

آب نباشد شناگر قابلی است.

92-He is like a scarecrow.

مثل لولوی سر خرمن می ماند.

93-Imitation can ruin people.

خلق را تقلیدشان بر باد داد

ای دو صد لعنت بر این تقلید باد

94-Seven wash basins, but no dinner.

آفتابه لگن هفت دست، شام و ناهار

هیچی.

95-His mustache is hanging.

سبیلش آویزان است.

96-The blind leading the blind.

کوری عصاکش کور دگر شود.

97-You can't carry two watermelons with one hand.

با یک دست دو هندوانه نمیشود برداشت.

98-It is the rotten tree that produces the worm.

کرم از خود درخت است.

99-His eyes are picking cherries.

چشمهایش آلبالو گیلاس می چیند.

100-To raise a snake in one's sleeve.

مار در آستین پروردن.

101-His hand reaches his mouth.

دستش به دهنش میرسد.

102-The neighbor's hen is a goose.

مرغ همسایه غاز است.

103-One can shut the town gates, but not people's mouths.

در دروازه را میشود بست در دهن مردم را

نمیشود.

104-Returning with hands longer than feet. (Being disappointed)

دست از پا درازتر برگشته.

105-The colander says to the slotted spoon, "you have too many holes!"

آبکش به کفگیر میگه تو چقدر سوراخ

داری.

106-The mouse was too big for the hole so it tied a broom to its tail!

موش تو سوراخ نمی رفت جارو بدمش می بست.

107-A handkerchief is not tied to a head which does not ache. (If it ain't broke don't fix it.)

سری را که درد نمی کنه دستمال نمی بندند.

108-When you raise the stick the thieving cat will flee.

چوب را که برداری گربه دزده فرار میکنه

109-Don't look a gift horse in the mouth.

دندون اسب پیش کشی را نمی شمرند.

110-My sweetheart has tied a rope around my neck, taking me wherever she wishes.

رشته ای بر گردنم افکنده دوست / میبرد هرجا که خاطرخواه اوست

111-It is as if his ships have sunk.

انگار کشتی هایش غرق شده.

112-An apple thrown into the air turns a thousand times before it falls.

یک سیب را بالا بیندازی هزار چرخ میخوره تا به زمین برسد.

113-To cut off your own root.

تیشه به ریشه خود زدن.

114-The tongue is the protector of the head.

زبان در دهان پاسبان سر است.

115-If you have money eat kabob, if you don't, smell it.

پولداران به کباب بی پولان به دود کباب.

116-The beard and the scissors are both in your hand.

ریش و قیچی هردو دست شماست.

117-There are mice in the walls, and mice have ears.

دیوار موش داره، موش هم گوش داره.

118-Who will tie the bell around the cat's neck?

حالا کیه که زنگوله را به گردن گربه بیندازه

119-It is as if she has come out of an elephants trunk.

انگار از دماغ فیل افتاده.

120-He had two legs and borrowed another two.

دو پا داشت دو پای دیگر هم قرض کرد.

121-To let the bouquet drift on water.

دسته گل به آب داده.

122-In one ear and out the other.

ازین گوش می شنود از آن گوش در میکند.

123-The cat who can't reach the meat, says "it stinks."

گربه دستش به گوشت نمیرسه میگه پیف پیف چه بو میده.

124-Having one hand in his bowl and one fist at his forehead.

دست در کاسه و مشت در پیشانی.

125-If the first brick is not set level, the wall will be crooked till the Pleiades.

خشت اول گر نهد معمار کج، تا ثریا میرود دیوار کج.

126-Say "no" once and not be burdened for nine months.

یک نه بگو و نُه ماه رو دل نکش.

127-Have I smelled my palm?

مگه کف دستم را بو کرده ام.

128-An arrow in the side of a young woman is better than having an old man by her side.

زن جوان را تیری در پهلو به که پیری.

129-Killing two birds with one stone.

با یک تیر دو نشان زدن.

130-A hump on top of another hump. قوز بالای قوز.

131-You cannot ride a camel and crouch.

شتر سواری دولا دولا نمیشه.

132-To put both feet in one shoe. (Being stubborn)

دو پا را در یک کفش کرده.

133-The chicken has one leg. (Stubborn person) مرغ یک پا داره.

134-Much as the snake hates the mint, it grows by its pit.

مار از پونه خوشش میاد، در لونه اش هم سبز میشه!

135-An excellent appearance, an empty pocket.

پز عالی جیب خالی.

136-God pity the beggar who begs from another beggar.

گدا به گدا رحمت به خدا.

137-His tears are in his
sleeves.

اشکش تو آستینش است.

138-Everyone gets struck by
electricity, I get struck by
lantern!

همه را برق میگیره ما را چراغ نفتی.

139-You may play, but not
with father's beard.

بازی بازی با ریش بابا هم بازی.

140-His elephant is thinking of
India. فیلش یاد هندوستان کرده.

142-Watch out! that our hats
don't get entangled.

بپا، کلاهمون تو هم نره.

143-He who climbs a ladder,
must begin at the bottom.

نردبام پله پله.

144-We have sifted our flour
and hung up the sieve.
(I am too old for this.)

ما آردمون را بیختیم و غربالمون را

آویختیم.

145-My ass had no tail since it
was a foal.

خَرِ ما از کُره گی دُم نداشت.

146-The lamp needed at
home should not be
donated to the mosque.

چراغی که به خانه رواست به مسجد حرام

است.

147-Where is the cat's
manners when the lid of
the pot is open.

در دیگ بازه حیای گربه کجاست.

148-A heart has a way to
another. دل به دل راه داره.

149-He who gives me small
gifts would have me live.

هر چه از دوست میرسد نیکوست.

150-Lucky in gambling,
unlucky in love.

کسی که در قمار شانس دارد در عشق

شانس ندارد.

151-To stab someone from
behind. از پشت به کسی خنجر زدن.

152-A knot that can be
opened with the hand
should not be opened with
the teeth.

گرهی که به دست باز میشود به دندان

نباید باز کرد.

153-To fan the flames.

میان دو کس جنگ چون آتش است

سخن چین بدبخت هیزم کش است.

154-An elephant and a cup.
(Two disproportionate
things)

فیل و فنجان.

155-Death comes once, so cry
only once. مرگ یکبار شیون هم

یکبار.

156-To play the oboe from the
wrong end.

سُرنا را از سر گشادش میزند.

157-It is a mistake to regret the
past. بر گذشته حسرت خوردن

خطاست.

158-Like an apple cut in half.

مثل سیبی که از وسط دونصف کرده

باشند.

159-What should I believe?
Your swearing or the cock's
tail.

قسم حضرت عباست را باور کنم یا دُم

خروس را.

160-It is like water poured on
fire. مثل آبی است که روی آتش

بریزی.

161-To embrace your knees in
sadness. زانوی غم به بغل گرفتن.

162-He who wants a peacock
must endure India.

۰هر که طاووس خواهد جور هندوستان

کشد.

163-A broken arm is a burden
to the neck.

دست شکسته و بال گردن است.

164-Who that goes softly, goes
safely.

آسه برو، آسه بیا که گربه شاخت نزنه.

165-When water rises above
one's head, it doesn't
matter whether a foot or a
hundred.

آب که از سر گذشت چه یک وجب چه

صد وجب.

166-Out of sight, out of mind.

از دل برود هر آنکه از دیده برفت.

167-Let your hat be your own
judge. کلاه خودت را قاضی کن.

168-To make cats dance.

گربه رقصانی کردن.

169-He is like a donkey stuck
in the mud. مثل خر تو گِل مونده.

170-Like mother like daughter.

نگاه به دست ننه کن مثل ننه غربیله کن.

171-No one will scratch my back but my fingernails.

کس نخارد پشت من جز ناخن انگشت من.

172-Too many cooks will spoil the broth.

آشپز که دوتا شد آش یا شور می شود یا بی نمک.

173-It is not eyeglasses that bring knowledge.

عینک سواد نمی آورد.

174-An old man's love ends in disgrace.

عشق پیری گر بجنبد سر به رسوایی زند.

175-The pen is mightier than the sword. قلم از شمشیر برنده تر است.

176-The fish is fresh whenever caught.

ماهی را هروقت از آب بگیری تازه است.

177-He that has been bitten by a serpent is afraid of a black and white rope. (Once bitten twice shy)

مارگزیده از ریسمان سیاه و سفید میترسد.

178-Reward for charity does not go far. صدقه راه دوری نمی رود.

179-An iron nail cannot pierce a stone. نرود میخ آهنین در سنگ.

180-Came out of the ditch and fell into the well.

از چاله درآمد و به چاه افتاد.

181-Put bread in the oven while it's hot.

تا تنور داغ است باید نان را چسباند.

182-It is merry when friends meet.

دوست را چیست به ز دیدن دوست.

# INDEX OF ENGLISH PROVERBS

روزمره و عامیانه گرفته شـده انـد.هـزار و یـک مثـل فارسـی-انگلیسـی، خصوصاً ویراسـت سوم آن از ویـــژه گـی هـایی برخـوردار اسـت کـه آنـرا از دیگـر کتابهای امثـال متمـایز میسازد. ۱-کتاب شامل امثال متـداول و رایـج میباشـد. ۲ - ترجمـه تحـت اللفظـی امثـال نـیز ارائه شده است تا درک امثـال فارسـی را بـرای انگلیسـی زبانـان آسـانتر سـازد. ۳ - فهرسـت کامل امثال در پایان کتاب آورده شده اسـت. ۴- بـرای توجـه بیشـتر، بیـش از صـد و هشتاد و سه مثل و اصطلاح معما گونـه تصویـر گردیـده اسـت و جـواب درسـت ایـن معمـا هـا در آخر کتاب و بر حسب شماره مثلها ارائه شـده. ۵ - از آنجـا کـه بسـیاری از خواننـدگـان ایـن کتاب آمریکـایی و یـا ایرانـی-آمریکـایی هسـتند و انگلیسـی زبان اولشـان مـی باشـد، در چاپ سوم تغییراتی داده شـده کـه کتـاب را بـرای ایـن دسـته از خواننـدگـان قـابل اسـتفاده بیشتر نماید. بهمین منظور ویراسـت سـوم «هـزار و یـک مثـل» از چـپ بـه راسـت مرتـب شده است. لطفاً نظرات و پیشنهادات خود را به نشـانی ناشـر یا نویسـنده ارسـال فرمـایید. بـا سپاس،

— سیمین ک. حبیبیان

**گروه ۱** - که برابرهای انگلیسی از جــهت صــورت ظــاهر و مفــهوم کــاملاً بــا امثـال فارسـی یکی است مــانند:

«در شهر کوران یک چشمی پادشاه است.»

"In the country of blind, the one eyed man is king."

و یا :

«با حلوا، حلوا، گفتن دهان شیرین نمیشود.»

"It is not by saying honey, honey,
that sweetness comes into mouth."

**گروه ۲** - آنـهایی کــه از جــهت ظــاهری و لغــوی تـا انـدازه ای متفاوت بـوده ولـی دارای یک مفهوم می باشـند مـانند:

«با دست پس میزند با پا پیش می کشد.»

"He refuses with the right hand and takes with the left."

**گروه ۳** - آنهایی که از جهت ظــاهر بسـیار متفـاوتند ولـی مفـهوم اصلـی آنـها یکـی است مـانند:

آســـوده کســـی کــه خــــر نـــدارد
از کــــاه و جـــواش خـــبر نـــدارد

"Little wealth, little care."

باید توجه داشت کـه مثل هـای انگلیسـی کــه در کتـاب آورده ام ترجمـه تحـت اللفظـی فارسی آنها نیست، بلکه مثل انگلیسی است که مشابه مثل فارسی مـی باشـد.

گاه برای یک مثل فارسـی چنـد مشابه انگلیسـی موجـود است، در ایـن مـوارد کوشـش شده است که نزدیکــترین مشابه انگلیسـی آن انتخـاب شـود. در تدویـن ایـن کتـاب سـعی گردیده که از منابع موثـق و مطمئـن اسـتفاده شـود. امـا در مـواردی هـم امثـال از مکالمـات

سرگرمی جالی برای همه خانواده میباشد. کوشش کرده ام که با مقایسه امثال انگلیسی و مشابه فارسی آنها هر چند کوچک جهت حفظ فرهنگ و زبان کشورمان در میان جامعه ایرانی و آمریکایی بردارم.

ما ایرانیها بر این عادت هستیم که پیوسته و گاه تعصب وار در روابط خود با جوانان، کلیه جوانب فرهنگ غربی را نفی میکنیم و همه را با یک چوب میرانیم. من کوشش کرده ام که بجای روند متداول و تأکید بر تفاوتها و برتری یک فرهنگ بر دیگری، بروی نکات مشترک و مشابه آنها از طریق مقایسه امثالشان تکیه کنم. من معتقدم که ضمن حفظ و گسترش فرهنگمان بجاست که به فرهنگ غرب و کشور میزبان خود نیز احترام گذارده و جنبه های مثبت آنرا تأکید کنیم.

در خاتمه وظیفه خود میدانم که از کلیه دوستانم که در چاپ اول و دوم کتاب مرا یاری دادند خصوصاً منوچهر آریانپور کاشانی، محمد علی ابوقداره، هادی بهار، حسن جوادی، جودی راسل، اسفندیار سپهری، فرهاد شیرزاد و فرهاد فلکی سپاسگزی کنم. جای آن دارد که از کلیه فروشگاههای ایرانی، نشریات، رادیو تلویزیونهای فارسی و امریکایی زبان برای حمایت از این کار فرهنگی قدردانی نمایم. برترین سپاسها را از خوانندگان گرامی این کتاب دارم که با پشتیبانی خود مرا در ارائه کارهای فرهنگی، اجتماعی دلگرم می نمایند.

لازم میدانم از همسرم دکتر محمد تقی حبیبیان که در نهایت شکیبایی مشوق من در امور فرهنگی و اجتماعی بوده است قدردانی نمایم. همچنین از فرزندانم پویا و مهتاب که مهمترین انگیزه من در تألیف این کتاب بوده اند سپاسگزارم.

## شیوه کار

بطور کلی سه گروه مشابه انگلیسی برای مثل های فارسی این فرهنگ وجود دارد:

دهد ولی راه خود را نمی داند چه مطلبی گویاتر از ایـن مثـل مـی تـوان گفـت: «کـل اگـر طبیب بودی سر خـود دوا نمـودی.

سیزده سال پیش که در اولین مدرسه زبان فارسی مریلند به تدریس پرداختم، عهده دار کارهـای فوق برنامه و نشریه ساده مدرسه نیز بودم. همواره کوشش مـی کردم چنـد مثـل سـاده را نیـز در نشریه بگنجانم و فرهنگ و زبان کشورمان را به دانش آمـوزان بیـاموزم. بـهمین روال همیشـه جواب سخنان شاگردان را با یک مثل فارسی و معادل انگلیسی آن پایان می دادم. از این روی من همیشه از بکار بردن و شنیدن امثال لذّت مـی بردم و بهمین سبب تصمیم گرفتم آنها را در کتـابی گرد آورم. فرهنگ موجود نتیجه بیش از سه سال و اندی کار و تحقیق مداوم روی این موضـوع است و شامل «هزار و یک مثل و اصطلاح» است.

مسلماً تعداد امثال فارسی که در زبان انگلیسی مشابه دارنـد بیـش از هـزار است، امّـا بایـد جایی و دلیلی برای پایان کار انتخـاب مـی کـردم. نقطـه پایـان را بـر مبنـای داسـتان هـای هـزار و یـک شب* قـرار دادم. و بـرای حسـن ختـام بیتـی مثـل گونـه سـروده ام:

یـــک هـــزار و یــــک مثـــل آورده ام

هـــر مثـــل گویـــا تـــر از صـــد داســـتان

May  "1001 Proverbs" bring you delight,
more than the stories of the "1001 Nights"

ضمن کار در مدرسه فارسی می دیدم که همراه کـردن تصویـر بـا امثـال، کمـک بـزرگی به یادگیری شاگردان می نمـاید بـهمین سبب امثـال انگلیسـی و مشـابه فارسـی آنـها را بـه صورت معما گونه درآورده ام کـه نـه تنـها آمـوزش را آسـانتر میکنـد بلکـه خـود

---

\* شهرزاد قصه گو هر شب به مدت هزار و یک شب برای خلیفه داستان زیبایی نقل کرده و بدین ترتیب خود را از مرگ می رهانید.

# آشنایی باهزار و یک مثل (ویراست سوّم)

چاپ اوّل این کتاب درمـــاه اوت ۱۹۹۶ میـلادی در ۷۰۰ نسخه منتشــر گردیــد و بـا اسـتقبال فراوان هم میهنان گرامـی و پشتیبانی رسانه هـای گروهـی مواجـه گشـت. طـی شـش مـاه کلیه نسخ آن به فروش رسید.ویراست دوم کتاب بـا تغییـرات بسـیار و بـا کیفیتـی برتـر در بیش از ۲۰۰۰ نسخه بـا همکـاری فرهـاد شـیـرزاد از IBEX   Publishers در اختیـار علاقمندان قـرار گرفـت و مجـدداً بـزودی نایـاب گردیـد. اینـک چـاپ سـوم کتـاب کـه همراه با تغییرات تازه ایست تقدیـم جامعـه ایرانـی و امریکـایی میگـردد.

این کتاب پیشکشی است به خانواده های ایرانی، بخصوص به جوانان بـرای ارتبـاط دو فرهنـگ ایرانی و غربی . «هزار و یک مثل» از یک سو جوانان را با جلوه هایی از فرهنـگ ایرانـی آشـنا میسازد و رابطه آنها را با این فرهنگ غنی و محیط خانواده همـوار مـی کنـد و از سـویی دیگـر تشـابه دیدگاههای ایرانی و غربی را که در مثل های روزمره بازتاب یافته نشان می دهد.

امثال آئینه فرهنگ و زندگی اجتماعی و تاریخی ملّت ها هستند و با چند کلمـــه کوتـاه مفهـوم وسیعی را در خاطر انسان زنده کرده و ادای مطلب مـی کننـد. بطوری که گفته اند، ضرب شمشیـر ندارد اثر ضرب مثل.

مثلاً زمانی که پشت سر کسی حرفهای بی اساس گفتــه مـی شـود چـه مطلبـی کوبنـده تـر ازین مثل فارسی است که می گویـد: «در دروازه را مـی شـود بسـت ولـی در دهـان مـردم را نمی شود.» و یا در مـورد کسـی کـه دیگـران را نصیحـت کـرده و راه و چـاه را نشـان مـی

دیپلماتیک و تعارفات سیاسی، ملت ها همیشه با هم «برادر» هستند و هیچوقت از در خواهری در نمی آیند، یادگار روزگارانی است که اتباع هر دو کشور، همه مردان سبیل کلفت بوده اند و معمولاً در مواقع اضطراری، از کشورثالثی، خواهر وارد می کرده اند.)

ملت ایران در ایامی که جیک جیک مستانش بود و فکر زمستانش نبود و غافل بود که سالی که نکوست از بهارش پیداست و نمیدانست که جوجه را آخر پاییز میشمرند، بجای اینکه یک ضرب المثل تابستانی به زبان خودش اضافه کند. ناگهان گز نکرده پاره کرد و چاه نکنده منار دزدید و آمد ابرویش را درست کند، چشمش را کور کرد و طوطی را گذاشت دهان قند.

پس از سال ۵۷،که متعاقباً صدها هزار و جمعاً یکی دو سه چهار میلیون که اکثریت از ورشکستگان به تقصیر و بی تقصیر بودند، به ممالک خارج کوچ کرده اند، اهمیت کتاب هزار و یک مثل فارسی-انگلیسی بیش از هر زمان دیگر احساس میشود.

کتاب حاضر با طراحی های شیرینی که چاشنی آن شده، میتواند تنقلی سرگرم کننده و آموزنده باشد. ضرب المثل ، مثل «کارتون» مرز نمی شناسد و حدودی را رعایت نمی کند. برای ما ایرانیان به غربت افتاده، مطالعه این کتاب، سفری است به اعماق فرهنگ و ادب عامه و سیر و سلوکی است در خلقیات مردمان ایران و آمریکا.

— هادی خرسندی

## ضرب المثل های بی مرز
## از هادی خرسندی

«ماما که دو تا بشه، ســر بچــه کـج در میاد!» ایـن، اولیـن ضـرب المثلـی بـود کـه شـنیدم. ازمادرم شنیدم. همیشه فکر میکنـم زن بیچـاره، وسـط چهـار درد زایمـان، اگـر ایـن ضـرب المثل را فریاد نزده بود، آن دو تا ماما، ســر مـرا کـج درآورده بودنـد.

امروز، مـن سـری صـاف دارم بـا دو تـا گـوش در دو طرفـش کـه از لحظـه دنیـا آمـدن، ضرب المثل شنیده اند و امیدوارم در آخرین لحظات زنـدگی هـم، بـاز بشـنوند:

انگـار داره گـوزو میـده، قبضـو میگیـره.

آره بابا، تا حالا هم از بـی کفنی زنده بـود.

ول کن بابا، فیل مرده و زنده اش صد تومنه.

یک ضرب المثل خوب گـاهی بـه انـدازه یـک کتـاب معنـی دارد و حتـی ممکـن اسـت بعضی مواقـع بـه انـدازۀ دو کتـاب و یـا بیشـتر معنـی داشـته باشـد.(بسـتگی دارد بـه تعـداد صفحات کتاب هـا.)

حالا وقتی مشابه این ضرب المثل ها به زبان انگیسی هم نوشـته شـود، چـه بسـا کـه بـاعث شود بچه های «خارجی» هم سرشان کج در نیاید. بخصـوص کـه در مغـرب زمیـن، بـه علـت پیشرفت های پزشکی، همیشه بیش از دو ماما بـالای سـر زائـو حضـور دارنـد.

حُسن دیگر مثلهای انگلیسی مشابه امثـال فارسـی، همـوار شـدن راه مبادلـۀ متلـک و نیـش و کنایه بین دو ملت دوست و برادر، ایران و آمریکـا خواهـد بـود. حتـی دو ملـت دوسـت و بـرادر، ایـران و انگلیـس هـم مـی تواننـد بـه تفـاهم بیشـتری برسـند.(ایـن کـه در اخبـار

# فهرست مندرجات

SIMIN HABIBIAN is a graduate of the College of Translation and of the Institute Français in Tehran, Iran. After leaving Iran in 1981, she began teaching Persian to young Iranians at the Iran-American Friendship Foundation in the Washington, D.C. area, where she found proverbs to be an effective teaching tool.

Simin has a deep interest in languages, cultures, and writing and has been very active in those areas. Simin spends her free time doing arts and crafts and writes for Persian language papers. She lives in Maryland with her husband. Simin likes to maintain important aspects of Persian cultural heritage, while building bridges with Western ways. She pursues this by emphasizing the similarities between the two cultures, using proverbs as a reflection of long-term traditions and experience.

*1001 Persian-English Proverbs* was first published in August 1996 and immediately became very popular in the Iranian-American community. It was sold out by January 1997. The second edition was published in April 1999 and was sold out by October 2000. These two editions were praised highly by the media and the reviewers. Numerous newspapers, radio programs and television shows, interviewed the author. *The Montgomery Gazette* called Simin Habibian "The Reigning Princess of Persian Proverbs" and "the Scheherzade of Proverbs." Simin was also interviewed by the Voice of America, BBC and various Iranian and American television programs.

This third edition goes beyond the previous two editions in several aspects. In particular, it includes major improvements to better accommodate the needs of those with English as their first language. As Simin has said:

*"May '1001 Proverbs' bring you delight,*
*more than the stories of the "1001 Nights"*

سیمین حبیبیان لیسانسیه زبان انگلیسی و ترجمه از مدرسه عالی ترجمه تهران و فارغ التحصیل انستیتو فرانسه است. او پس از چند سال تدریس در مدارس تهران، در آخرین سفر خود به امریکا در سال ۱۹۸۱ در ایالت مریلند ماندگار شد. سیمین مدت چهار سال به تدریس زبان فارسی به کودکان انگلیسی زبان ایرانی پرداخت و عهده دار فعالیت های فوق برنامه نیز بود. او مـدت دو سال نیز در کلاس های ESOL برای بزرگسالان انگلیسی تدریس کرده است. سیمین به کارهای اجتماعی و فرهنگی دلبستگی خاصی دارد و همیشه در این زمینه فعال بـوده اسـت. او اوقـات فراغت خود را به کارهای دستی گوناگون نوشتن و تهیه گزارش بـرای نشـریات مـی پـردازد. «هزار و یک مثل» نتیجه بیش از سه سال کار مداوم سیمین در ایـن زمینـه اسـت. وی در بـارۀ کتابش میگوید:

«یک هزار و یک مثل آورده ام

هر مثل گویا تر از صد داستان»

May "1001 Proverbs" bring you delight,
more than the stories of the "1001 Nights."


## هزارو یک مثل فارسی ـ انگلیسی در رسانه های گروهی

چاپ دوم هزار و یک مثل مانند چاپ اول آن با استقبال بی نظیری روبـرو گردیـد. بسیاری از نشریات، رادیو تلویزیون های فارسی زبان کتاب را معرفی و با سیمین مصاحبه نمودند. روزنامـه گازت در دو نوبت صفحه‌ای‌را به معرفی «هزار و یک مثل» و نویسنده آن اختصاص داد. روزنامه گازت در عنوان های مقاله های خود به سیمین لقب «پرنسس امثال فارسی» و «شهرزاد مثل گو» داد. تلویزیون انگلیسی زبان منطقه مریلند همچنین رادیو هـای بی‌بی‌سی و صـدای آمریکـا بـا نویسنده مصاحبه کردند. چند نشریه داخل کشور نیز در باره موفقیت ایـن کتـاب نوشـتند. ایـن کتاب در کتابخانه بسیاری از مراکز تحقیقاتی و دانشگاههای جهان و برخـی از کتابخانـه هـای عمومی امریکا موجود است.

# هزار و یک مثل

# فارسی‌ـ انگلیسی

### ویراست سوّم

گردآوری و تصاویر از

سیمین ک. حبیبیان

پیشگفتار از

هادی خرسندی

چاپ پاژن